Till Death Do Us Part

The story of my wife's fight with lung cancer

by

Bob Urman

"It is ever so much more wonderful

to love than to be loved..."

- Linda Urman, 1966

Contents

.

Introduction

This is the story of my wife Linda's ten-month battle with lung cancer.

The basic cast of characters includes Linda, myself, and our two sons—Mike and Dan. Others mentioned include Chris, my sister-in-law; Karyn, her daughter; and Jane, her best friend from childhood.

Linda's story is told via the journal posts I wrote on the CaringBridge web site, starting when she first entered the hospital for emergency surgery, and ending with her memorial service.

- - -

It all started when Linda noticed a small lump on her neck, and her primary doc suggested she have it removed and biopsied. Simultaneously, although she had long been walking several miles a day with friends, she began feeling somewhat winded during her walks.

She called me at work after receiving the news about the biopsy—adinocarcinoma—and said, "Come home. I'm scared."

Neither of us realized at the time that the cancerous lump was the tip of the iceberg—a metastasized area far from the source.

But the doctors knew what it meant, and had her get a scan.

By the time she went in to have the biopsy stitches removed, she was so weak I had to take her there in a borrowed wheelchair. The scan results showed that the cancer was everywhere, and, since she had some blood clots in her legs, she needed immediate surgery to install a filter.

While that was happening, I met with the oncologist. After reviewing her scan results, his first words were, "No one can survive this."

That is where the story begins.

Journal

SATURDAY, SEPTEMBER 26, 2009, 6:02 PM

Linda is in room 3110 at Alexian Brothers Medical Center in Elk Grove. She has a lung clot and cancer in her lung, liver, bones, and brain.

They are trying to determine if the brain lesions will disallow the use of heparin to shrink the clot, which is hampering her breathing. She did have about a liter of fluid drained from in/around her lungs, so she's breathing better than she was, but she's still on oxygen.

There is hope she will come home for a while and, possibly with some chemotherapy, be able to function for a while longer, but until the consequences of the brain lesions are known, nothing is certain.

What is certain is that she values your friendship and would appreciate hearing from you in any format—phone, visit, comments here.

SATURDAY, SEPTEMBER 26, 2009, 7:33 PM

They (Linda has a committee of 5: primary doctor, surgeon, pulmonary specialist, neurologist, and oncologist) have decided it's OK to do direct injections of heparin (instead of IV) to reduce the clot without risking any brain bleeding, so that will begin at some point soon. She had a good nap this afternoon and is now able to sleep on her side (which is her preference) as well as her back.

MONDAY, SEPTEMBER 28, 2009, 4:45 AM

As of 2:30 AM, Linda's blood pressure was low and she was moved to intensive care. She still has fluid around her heart, so they will be doing an echocardiogram as soon as possible. They've had some trouble with her veins, so they are putting in a central line. We were told she was awake and alert, and we are waiting to see her.

MONDAY, SEPTEMBER 28, 2009, 5:13 AM

They've performed the echocardiogram and are going to drain some of the fluid around her heart. This procedure should take less than an hour, so we may know more then. I forgot to mention that while they are getting ready to do the draining we do get to hold her hand, talk with her, and let her know we're here.

MONDAY, SEPTEMBER 28, 2009, 1:05 PM

Linda is doing SO much better. She had another 3/4 liter of fluid drained from her lungs and is now breathing almost normally again. She's eating lunch, and spent time talking with her coworkers.

They are still trying to figure out where the fluid is coming from, or why, so they can stop it permanently.

MONDAY, SEPTEMBER 28, 2009, 11:13 PM

Linda is still slowly filling up with fluid, but more slowly now, and her last X-ray wasn't too bad. Hopefully she won't need to be tapped again tonight. She actually got about a 3-1/2 hour nap this afternoon. The next steps are to:

1. Get her stabilized as far as fluid buildup is concerned, which may involve installing a drain or drains, and

2. Get radiation therapy for her brain tumors. That is a 10-day series of X-ray treatments intended to shrink the tumors. They'll continue to shrink for two to three weeks after the treatment ends, and then she can get rescanned. The treatment is general in the beginning, i.e., the whole brain, but if after the first treatment there are some small remaining tumors, they can be specifically targeted with more precision (using what's called a gamma knife).

3. Once the radiation treatment is done, she can consider chemotherapy.

All of these things are to improve her quality of life and possibly extend her survival time; none are cures.

Thanks so much to everyone who has posted. They have been a great comfort to her. I've read the posts to her and she has been touched and amazed at all the people who responded—people that she hasn't heard from for many years but who still remember her fondly, which is definitely the way she remembers them.

I've asked her about all the previous boyfriends, and she just said she likes to collect them.

TUESDAY, SEPTEMBER 29, 2009, 11:49 AM

Linda slept well last night—she was only awakened once. She is still breathing OK today and is now scheduled for radiation this afternoon.

I forgot to mention that Dan came in last night. She was definitely happy to see him. He has been great, and is here to help as well as he can and as long as necessary. He will be a great help in allowing us to rotate our time between being here and getting back to work for a while. Dan brought Linda a California hat for her radiation and plans to read her science fiction stories.

Also, since lunch yesterday, her blood sugar has been low enough that they haven't needed to give her insulin.

We read her all the new posts this morning. They are so wonderful and she says to say that she can feel everyone's friendship and concern and they really help. I start with the name of the person first, and she says that while I'm reading, she's hearing the person's voice. (That's good, because reading these aloud is always pretty emotional for me and my voice isn't always too steady.)

TUESDAY, SEPTEMBER 29, 2009, 6:11 PM

They started prepping Linda for radiation therapy today. This was not physically hard, but kind of stressful, and they ended up by temporarily abandoning her in a hallway. They thought she was going to be transferred out of Intensive Care, so when she got back to her room it was stripped, and they stuck her in a half-made bed with no call button.

They're keeping her in the ICU tonight because she's going to have surgery tomorrow to install drains to drain the heart and lung fluid as much as possible. These will actually end up in physical tubes coming out of her and they will stay there until the draining stops, which is estimated to be a few days.

After the surgery, when they think it's appropriate, they will transfer her from the ICU to Telemetry, where vitals are checked a bit less frequently, so hopefully she can get some more sleep.

Because of the surgery, tomorrow will probably not be a good visiting day.

It was hard to hear that she was abandoned and we felt bad that we weren't there, but when we got home tonight she had left a phone message that they had given her a nice bath and put skin cream on her and surrounded her with pillows and she's very comfortable now.

All three of us were there today, as well as Chris and Karyn, and a few other visitors. Dan will be there in the morning tomorrow, and Mike and I will show up later, after the surgery.

Due to the surgery, the radiation treatments will probably not start for another day or so.

WEDNESDAY, SEPTEMBER 30, 2009, 9:05 AM

I spoke with the nurse at 6 this morning. She said that Linda got a sleeping pill and slept very well. Obviously, she's a little concerned and nervous about the upcoming surgery. Dan should be with her now; I'll be there shortly after the surgery and Mike should get there a little later.

WEDNESDAY, SEPTEMBER 30, 2009, 1:20 PM

Linda had to wait for her surgery to start, but she went in around 12:30 and it should be about an hour, then we'll wait till she's out of recovery.

She had a good morning and felt reasonable. Dan read to her, and they watched some YouTube videos together.

Dan was telling me she talked with the medical oncologist this morning and he was pretty optimistic that she'd be going home soon, and when she said, "You mean in a couple weeks?" he said if everything goes OK it would be considerably sooner than that. He said she ought to be able get up and move around some as well. After the recovery she will be moved from whatever ICU she has been in (strange that I don't know—I didn't know there is more than one) to the CVICU (Cardiovascular ICU). I don't know for sure but assume it's because the surgery today is being done by a cardiac and thoracic surgeon. Anyone intending to visit should park near the Brock building, go up to the 1st floor, and look for signs to the CVICU.

OK. The surgeon just came and said Linda did really well. They got a lot of fluid out and she now has three drains—one for each lung and one for the heart. The drains will stay in until she "runs dry," which should be in three to five days; the surgeon said that after they are removed, scar tissue will form, which will inhibit further buildup. What wonderful news.

The surgeon has some minor concerns about starting radiation therapy, which could interfere with the healing process, but still says it may be as early as tomorrow. I'm starting to think she may actually get out of here soon, and both of us can't wait for that.

We don't know what will be needed at home (oxygen?) but whatever it is, with Mike and Dan's help, we'll cope.

WEDNESDAY, SEPTEMBER 30, 2009, 8:59 PM

Linda came out of surgery and was in her room about 3:30 PM. She had some pain where the incision was (and, I think, where the drain tubes were coming out) so they gave her a pain reliever, then some muscle relaxant, which really did the trick. She fell asleep about 6 PM. As of a few minutes ago, she was still sleeping and her numbers were looking fine.

They expect some soreness tomorrow, but all in all today was a good day.

Having Dan around has been a fantastic help, to us and to her. She says she has been helped by our presence, and Dan made the morning go by without worrying about the upcoming surgery. Mike has continued to provide solid support, and has been keeping an eye on me as well. Both Mike and Dan have been great, and are obviously a testament to her as a parent. I can't thank them enough.

THURSDAY, OCTOBER 1, 2009, 1:05 PM

Linda was much better this morning; she got a good amount of sleep. She got another bath and her hair washed early, and she's now eating lunch. Since radiation is going to start today, we're waiting for that. Each treatment is supposed to be five minutes or so, but she has to be transported there and back. This time I'll be with her all the way.

Dan has been with her this morning as usual and is now on his lunch break.

So far I've been able to go to work in the morning, which helps keep me in the loop.

THURSDAY, OCTOBER 1, 2009, 6:29 PM

Linda is out of the ICU, in Telemetry—more of a standard room. She's still on pain meds, but I think it's getting better. She had her first radiation treatment today, and was pretty nervous going in, but came out in five minutes much more relaxed and said it was easy. They will be giving her a cortisone-based steroid during the treatment to prevent swelling, so she doesn't have a two-week headache, but it will push her sugar up a bit. Her sugar had been hovering from 150 to just under 200 the past day and a half, which meant she didn't need insulin. But I guess that's a small issue in the grand scheme.

Her fluid draining is progressing well. I don't understand the equipment, but they've moved to a less aggressive suctioning, so I assume that's good. She was tired, so we left her to sleep a while, then maybe she'll get dinner, and then sleep some more.

We are clinging to the hope that there will be a somewhat more normal period where she can walk a little and still breathe OK. She did say it was a treat that she actually sat in a chair for a while this morning.

As always, Mike and Dan have been great. Dan has been spending mornings with her. He's been calm and observant, was taking notes about when she last had pain meds so the next doses wouldn't be missed, and was making sure she was following instructions to drink a lot of water because (I forgot to mention initially) they've been able to remove her main line. When she got to her new room, the first thing he did was to bring back two cups of water. He'll be with her for her next radiation treatment tomorrow morning, and we'll see what happens next.

FRIDAY, OCTOBER 2, 2009, 6:13 AM

Linda slept well in her new room. Another piece of medical equipment was removed early in the evening (I'm not supposed to mention what it was) but she is now forced to get out of bed and walk to the washroom in her room. Her nurse James (she said, "Ooh, I have a GUY nurse") told me she did well, and without oxygen on the way, although she did get the oxygen back afterwards.

I've talked about how great Dan has been, but haven't said enough about Mike. He has certainly been emotionally affected as any of us, but has been a steady help. He comes home and prepares (and makes sure we eat) a decent dinner (when we don't go out), cleans up (he says that is part of his therapy), and thinks of the small things that I haven't. The most recent example: When Linda was in the ICU, some friends sent in some beautiful flowers, but we were told they weren't allowed in ICU and we'd have to take them home. This morning I found a note on my briefcase

11

reminding me that she was now out of ICU. Could she have the flowers now? I checked, and it's fine, and Dan will be bringing them back in today.

Both Mike and Dan are putting up pretty well with my obsessively trying to plan for all eventualities (without having a clue of what they might be). They keep telling me "Don't worry yet; we have time to get this figured out."

They were also a great help in my getting to sleep last night. I just sat and listened to them talk computer/video game speak to each other, and pretty soon I began to drift off.

FRIDAY, OCTOBER 2, 2009, 9:30 AM

She just saw the cardiologist, and if her latest chest X-ray is OK, they'll be removing the drain tubes today. I'm keeping everything crossed.

FRIDAY, OCTOBER 2, 2009, 10:54 AM

Two radiation treatments down, eight to go. She's taking a nap and I'll be heading there in about an hour. There still must be some fluid left to come out; they want to keep the tubes in until Monday or so. I assume that means she won't come home until after that, but don't know.

FRIDAY, OCTOBER 2, 2009, 5:34 PM

We've seen a lot of people today. A couple visitors, several doctors, nurses, a patient representative, the social worker, the chaplain...

I've been comforted quite a bit (and I hope Linda has as well) by the extent of support I now know is out there. Linda now has a prayer blanket and has officially been blessed. There are places in Schaumburg that loan some medical equipment, there are vouchers available to help with various non-covered costs, but mostly it's knowing there are people to lean on for help if necessary. The cardiologist nurse already has discussed follow-up visits after she is discharged, and we're told the pulmonary people will as well.

And that's in addition to the many offers of help we've received from all our friends and family.

So we won't be out there alone.

SATURDAY, OCTOBER 3, 2009, 10:50 AM

Dan went to be with her this morning as usual. He let me and Mike sleep in a little, and I had a few things that had to be done this morning. (We'll be going in soon.) But every day is a step forward and I am amazed at how far she's come since last Monday. When I called this morning she answered right away with a bright "Hi," said she was sitting in her chair and, wonder of wonders, no oxygen. Yeah, it was nearby, but the fact that she didn't need it at the moment is great.

Writing this journal is very strange. It's amazing how easy it is to bare your soul. Dan, who used to write a personal blog, says it's a common reaction and, based on some study or other, has to do with the anonymity. Maybe so, but my feeling is that I know that everyone who is likely to be reading this is a friend and will be understanding and supportive. And that has certainly been the case so far. Besides, this isn't really about me, it's about Linda and her friends and family.

I seem to be forgetting a lot of small things right now— usually little tasks that (if you can excuse some engineering- type analogies) are down in the noise and not really part of the signal, like depositing a check, but I don't want to forget to talk about Mike and Dan's help. And I did forget to mention Dan's comment from yesterday, which went something like, "You and Mike have your full-time jobs; being with Mom is mine."

The other thing that we learned yesterday from the thoracic oncology coordinator (a wonderful woman who described much of the support I mentioned yesterday) is that, after smoking, the second leading cause of lung cancer is radon. They are going to include a radon test kit along with their information packet. I know we tested some years ago, and found nothing, but she said that the recommendation now is to test every two years. So do your radon testing.

SATURDAY, OCTOBER 3, 2009, 6:42 PM

While Dan was there this morning, a couple of his friends showed up and one brought flowers. What amazing and caring friends he has.

We arrived around 12:30 PM to find her finishing lunch. She was up in her chair the whole time, and, although she didn't feel the need for oxygen, was one percentage point lower than they wanted her to be in saturation (93% instead of 94%) so she was using it when we arrived. But the flow rate, which had usually been at 4 liters per minute, and up to 6 when she was having more trouble, was down to 1. (They measured her saturation when they took her for an X-ray to check her fluid buildup levels.)

She saw friends, talked and joked with them and us, and finally got tired and back into her bed around 4 PM, and we left so she could nap. Mike and I went shopping and Dan went home, where we discovered on our arrival that he must have been exhausted because he's still asleep.

I just talked to her a little bit ago, and she had some news—she's getting the main chest tube (the one for her heart) removed tonight, as they are pretty sure that part is done draining. That's the larger tube, so at least she can start healing where that was. She still will have the two lung drains for a little longer, probably until Monday. She has so many doctors on her team we've lost count, but the cardiac specialist said as far as her heart was concerned, she could be discharged any time.

Mike is making dinner—Dan requested tofu stir-fry, and Mike is also making me some guacamole—pretty nice of him since he's basically allergic to avocado.

The way things are looking, we'd better do some house cleaning tomorrow. It's probably the only chance we'll get. I never looked forward to that chore before.

SATURDAY, OCTOBER 3, 2009, 8:34 PM

So: getting tired, last update today. Her cardiac chest tube is out and she's happy about that. That tube was connected to a briefcase-sized box on the floor, so the only tether she has now is the oxygen. (The lung tubes have their own small drain receptacles at their ends and go wherever she goes.)

A side note: I should mention Dan's website. It is pretty specific to video game aficionados, but is a great example of his writing, which is much better than mine, and better than most I've seen. This was just recently started, so it will be obvious why there's not as much content as he would have preferred, but the site (and his preferred critical essay) is at

http://www.pixelpoppers.com/2009/09/play-me-story-part-one-metal-gear-solid.html

SUNDAY, OCTOBER 4, 2009, 6:41 PM

Another pretty good day today. Linda had more visitors and received some beautiful plants, a fantastic vase with a "fall arrangement"—some fall grasses and other things, I think, but beautifully arranged by the giver with the thought that this is something that will last. We are going to enjoy it for a long time. The plants were quite interesting as well—small yellow and red flowers—even Linda (who started out as a botany major) wasn't familiar with them. And she also got a warm and fuzzy set of slippers, which will be perfect in her room and when she comes home now that we're moving into fall.

The best part of the day for her, however, may have been that she got to have her hair washed for real—not the stuff they apply and comb out sitting in bed. She just luxuriated in that treatment—said they rubbed her back and everything.

Coming home is getting more and more real. There is still some drainage from the lung tubes, which will determine the final date, but we're starting to think that as soon as Tuesday is a possibility. She's looking forward to it and a little apprehensive at the same time. She said that once she's home, her physical limitations will be more obvious. But those limitations should diminish for a while, at least, after the chemo—that's the hope we're clinging to.

MONDAY, OCTOBER 5, 2009, 9:57 PM

I've been in town just over a week now, and over that week I've had the great pleasure of seeing my mother get better and stronger every day. I made a comment to my father at one point that I considered hanging out with Mom at the hospital to be my new full-time job, and I can tell you it's easily the most rewarding job I've ever had.

We have a lot of fun, talking and watching YouTube videos together. I'm always a little disappointed when the afternoon comes and my father and brother show up, because then I don't have her all to myself anymore.

As great as the people at the hospital have been, I'm definitely looking forward to her coming home tomorrow. It's going to make things easier on everyone and I'm sure she'll be more comfortable. Plus we can step up from YouTube to DVDs, since I have a stack of movies I'm planning to make her watch with me. I really want to see what she thinks of the new Star Trek movie.

-Dan

TUESDAY, OCTOBER 6, 2009, 9:07 PM

It's been a long day, but now she's home. We're all exhausted, and it's time to learn to deal with this next phase. We will update as appropriate, but probably not quite as often as before.

As always, you can contact us by phone or email.

WEDNESDAY, OCTOBER 7, 2009, 7:13 PM

Linda had a great day today. She really has perked up quite a bit since being home. She says it may have something to do with no drain tubes, no lights all night, and no staff coming at her with blood pressure cuffs or needles.

She was evaluated for oxygen need before we left yesterday and did very well—she was well above the threshold after her "exercise" walk down the hall. However, she did have an emotional need to know that oxygen was available if she needed it, so, after a lot of paper work we came home with a portable tank. The time she expected to need it was on her way to her radiation treatment, but although they carried it in the car, she didn't use it at all. Now she knows she doesn't need to have it in the car either. But we'll keep it until we find out what is involved with getting the chemo treatments.

We had been given and were storing a wheelchair, so we dragged it out and took her on what used to be our normal three-mile walk. She thought it was great, and we learned that it isn't quite as easy as it looks to go up and down the sidewalks with its bumps and hills that are normally not even noticed. It was a great workout for us and a good time out for her.

She is getting her legs and balance back and should be able to go on short walks soon and maybe longer walks later.

Friday will be the first of her follow-up appointments, so we'll have a better idea of the immediate future after that.

Even though for twelve nights I got used to hogging all the blankets and turning on lights whenever I wanted, it's so great to have her home.

FRIDAY, OCTOBER 9, 2009, 5:57 PM

Linda continues to be overwhelmed by the gifts, comments, and support of her many friends. (She keeps telling me, "I'm just not that nice a person.")

But she is very grateful (as am I) and it all helps to keep the scarier parts more in the background, which is where we want them for now.

She will start chemo on Monday the 19th. She will have a port installed prior to that, and the treatments, if everything goes as planned, will be once every three weeks for six weeks. For each of those three-week slots the middle week will be the one where her blood counts and platelets will be more suppressed and she'll be most susceptible to anemia, colds, etc. So we will learn what to watch out for and hope for the best.

I'm always impressed by her positive attitude. Every once in a while we get sad and hold each other and cry for a while, but more often she has a smile and is enjoying the good parts. At the moment she's watching a DVD and deciding where we are to take her for dinner.

SATURDAY, OCTOBER 10, 2009, 6:35 PM

Today we got some papers signed, took her picture, and she finished watching the Pride & Prejudice DVD.

She had more visitors, which meant more food and gifts. One of her friends is in the later stages of chemotherapy herself, and she and her husband have a lot of experience to share. They are so positive and optimistic that even with the realities of the upcoming treatment they were a big help psychologically and have us believing that anything is possible.

We had another walk-and-roll (shorter—it got cold out there) around the local pond. While she is napping, Mike is dealing with the whole mackerel he bought. (Dinner tonight will be interesting—mackerel with lemon and personally delivered homemade soup.) Dan is researching more videos to entertain her with, and I'm doing this blog as therapy. At least she's sleeping—the steroid evidently makes that more difficult. And although she was tapering off now that the radiation treatments are finishing, she'll be on it again for the chemo.

Tomorrow a group of her friends from Bloomington/Normal are coming to meet her for lunch and spend a few hours here, and she is looking forward to that.

SUNDAY, OCTOBER 11, 2009, 4:45 PM

Today Linda had a great time. Her Bloomington high school girlfriends came up and spent the afternoon, during which she got more phone calls and another visitor with a "prescription" gift pack. Mike, Dan, and I went for our walk while Linda and her friends went back in time.

She started the morning out by terrorizing me (right now, it doesn't take much to do that) because she became very lightheaded every time she sat up or stood up or even when she raised an arm to reach for her floss. I called our doctor and while awaiting his call back, I called our neighbor, a nurse. She came over and took Linda's blood pressure and confirmed it was pretty low, which kind of took us back to her crashing and being transferred to the ICU a week ago. But Linda said there was no problem breathing, and our neighbor said her heart and breathing sounded OK. The doctor had her stop her blood pressure meds, and after she had some food and juice began to feel better. Then Mike made his promised French toast; she liked that a lot.

By early afternoon the lightheadedness was gone, so she was able to enjoy the afternoon.

Our neighbor, another of Linda's wonderful friends, said she'd come by this evening to do one more check.

Next week will be the last three radiation treatments, and then getting her "port" installed. I'm hoping things will go relatively smoothly.

MONDAY, OCTOBER 12, 2009, 12:57 PM

This morning Linda had me get up and bring her some breakfast cereal before I left, and she sat up on the edge of the bed to eat it. Since I wasn't going to be with her, I was a little concerned about her blood pressure and asked her how she felt. She got this big grin, raised both arms above her head, and said, "Look! Look!"

Needless to say, I left feeling better.

TUESDAY, OCTOBER 13, 2009, 6:44 PM

I have to leave a couple hours earlier than usual tomorrow (I'm going out of town for work) so I came home a little early to help finish getting her records in order for her next appointments. Tomorrow is the last radiation and Thursday she gets a port installed. I've been trying to think of some witty port-related comments or jokes, but haven't come up with much (or anything) so far—so help is hereby solicited.

Small things can make "normal" activity a lot better. We had a shower seat, but it was just large enough that the shower door hit it when closing. So I found a smaller one yesterday, and it's made her life that much easier. It's also lighter, which helps when she has to lift it out of the shower and move it over to the sink.

We got the records organized, and were able to get in a couple walk-and-roll laps around our pond before dark.

THURSDAY, OCTOBER 15, 2009, 8:59 PM

I got an early flight home today, and made it to the hospital waiting room just as they were looking for a family member. She was feeling reasonably good, and finally had some food (they had made her go without food or drink for 15 hours prior to the surgery) and we took her home.

She now has the port. And thanks for the port jokes, etc., since she did read all those while I was away.

More presents and cards have arrived. Everyone has been so wonderful and caring, and she still can't get over the support she's received. I found out that her boss told her that at DeVry (where she taught) they have never before seen such a response—coworkers and students alike asking about her progress and sending their good wishes.

For many years, Linda has been part of a monthly gathering of neighbor (and ex-neighbor) women where the excuse is playing bingo but the real motive is to visit and talk. The bingo group's get-together was scheduled for tonight, and Linda really wanted to be able to go. I dropped her off a couple of hours ago, and am somewhat amazed (and very glad) that she hasn't yet called to be brought home. Good friends are amazing therapy, and she needs and deserves every bit of that help now. So, although I didn't have anything to do with it, thanks (again) for that continuing support.

SATURDAY, OCTOBER 17, 2009, 8:42 AM

Linda's "almost sister" Jane and her husband Andy arrived last night after a long drive from their home in Missouri. Although it was late and Linda was tired, she was obviously glad to see Jane.

She has had more difficulty with leg strength than she expected, and when she saw her primary doc to check out an earache, he told her she had been through quite a lot and was expecting too much too soon. But she's frustrated and her legs hurt and she tires easily. We are all hoping that the course she is on will help.

We got our radon test results. We had tested quite a few years ago and found no problems. But the results of improving our windows and upgrading our siding insulation are that we are now over the limit in the test—almost at twice the "corrective measures" limit. Now we are supposed to do a second (or confirmation) test. Assuming that will come out the same, I will start investigating mitigation techniques next week. Anyone wishing to read more on radon can go to http://www.radon.com.

MONDAY, OCTOBER 19, 2009, 12:56 PM

Jane and Andy left Sunday morning. Despite the fact that they had to leave early so they could get home and do their prep for their Monday morning classes, which meant we had to be up by 6 AM, it was great that they came and spent time with us. We're hoping that when Linda gets better we'll be able to go back to Missouri to visit them again.

Linda felt better last evening and even better and stronger this morning. She was somewhat apprehensive about the chemotherapy, so I went in with her this morning (in addition to Dan, who will stay with her all day). They took some blood and found her hemoglobin was a little low, which explains her fatigue. After she got in and saw the environment (comfy reclining chair, close bathroom, assuring nurses) she felt fine and told me I could leave.

We now have an appointment on Wednesday afternoon with a radon mitigating contractor for an appraisal and estimate. Evidently the strategy is to bore a hole into the slab and route a pipe up through the attic and outside the house where a fan will provide suction to pull the air from under the slab, which is the radon source. The preliminary cost guesstimate was $1200, which I thought was cheap for what it was avoiding.

We'll see how Linda does the next few weeks as the chemo does its work. My biggest job is to avoid getting sick and avoid any people who are sick—I'm planning an 18-week moratorium on handshaking.

MONDAY, OCTOBER 19, 2009, 7:10 PM

I came home to find Linda reading and smiling at me as I came in. She had a good day and everything worked easily and well—she is very happy to have her port. She was also happy to have some of the things provided by one of her more experienced friends—a hat kept her head warm and a blanket kept her feet warm. Dan provided his usual entertainment, and went to Steak 'n Shake and brought back lunch for her. She used the excuse to get a double chocolate fudge milkshake—the first time she's had a milkshake in years.

Now we'll see how she does over the next few days. She doesn't have to go back for three weeks, but in between will be follow-up visits with the lung surgeon, the cardiac specialist, the family doctor, etc. And tomorrow she gets her wig—she's decided to be blonder—so I'll have a new surprise when I get home.

TUESDAY, OCTOBER 20, 2009, 3:03 PM

Linda went in and got her wig today. She had two choices and opted for the slightly darker blond because everyone said it matched her complexion better and Dan said it made her look ten years younger. The picture is up on the photos page: if you have trouble finding it, look for the younger chick.

So far, other than being somewhat tired, she feels OK, which is great—no nausea or fetal curling or personality changes. Her more experienced friend said that the third day was the worst for her, so we'll wait until tomorrow is over to judge.

THURSDAY, OCTOBER 22, 2009, 6:06 PM

Delayed update:

Tuesday afternoon: I was so proud of Linda—she took a stand and controlled her life.

She had gone in for an ultrasound for suspected blood clots in her leg. They were confirmed. They told her she would be admitted and treated (typical in normal circumstances). Knowing she cannot have blood thinners now, she told them "No, I won't." So they tried to reach her oncologist, and finally reached his on-call partner, who, not having Linda's records immediately available, told them to take her to the emergency room.

She took one look at the emergency room, saw a roomful of sick kids, and said, "I refuse treatment and I'm leaving," which she did. When we finally got in touch with the on-call doctor, who by this time *did* have her records, he told her she made the right decision.

After she was home and was able to get her feet up again, and we all calmed down a bit, she felt better.

As of today, the most obvious effect she's feeling from the chemo is that she fatigues easily and is somewhat tired most of the time. Her hemoglobin was somewhat low, and next week we'll see whether that needs to be addressed further.

In the meantime at home we now have an appointment to get our radon issue taken care of, and by Thanksgiving it should be done. I learned that radon readings in our area have been higher than usual this year, and the best explanation is that since we have had a lot of rain, the ground water level is higher than normal. I'm hoping that means that we haven't been at present levels for very long—certainly not over the summer as we keep the house pretty ventilated and run a fan at night.

Once the work is done we will retest.

SATURDAY, OCTOBER 24, 2009, 9:39 AM

Linda's echocardiogram on Friday was good—no fluid, and her heart looks better than a couple weeks ago. Her main issue is low blood pressure, leading to being lightheaded. The low BP is caused by the cancer dilating the blood vessels and fluid pooling uselessly in her legs and feet. So she visited the oncologist's office, where they used her port to fill her with saline, and that helped a lot. Then they told her to start drinking Gatorade, which should help keep her blood pressure up. She'll be doing that this weekend and be rechecked Tuesday; if that isn't enough they can give her some meds to re-constrict the blood vessels.

At least she hasn't had any nausea—only some reflux a couple of times. She does have to eat and drink slowly, but she's getting used to that.

SATURDAY, OCTOBER 24, 2009, 6:15 PM

Yes, the sun did come out, and all of a sudden Linda asked to be taken for a walk. Mike was deep into a team-player game and couldn't go, but Dan and I bundled her up and went out. The Gatorade (she is to drink two 20-ounce bottles per day and is mostly finished with today's dose) seems to be working, as she walked out to the car and later walked back in and wasn't lightheaded. I posted two pictures from the walk.

The hat she's wearing was her father's—he bought it on a trip to Alaska. It is very soft and very warm. Sally—if you are reading this—Linda wants to know if you remember what it's made of.

SUNDAY, OCTOBER 25, 2009, 8:27 PM

Today was a quiet restful day. Linda napped and read, and Mike and I got in some yard work. The best part was in the afternoon when a friend and her husband came over to visit. Her friend is so optimistic and positive it affects us all. And the great food and beer they brought affected us as well—we devoured quite a bit of it.

Linda has managed to drink her allotment of Gatorade for two days now, and the lightheadedness has been kept to a minimum, so the Gatorade seems to be doing its job. She isn't always very hungry, but is trying to keep eating when she can. After dinner we watched an episode of Glee, a program she's been enjoying, and she went to bed. Tomorrow starts with early breakfast and then I'll be back at work.

I keep thinking how lucky we are to have Dan here. Mike has been wonderful, and I'm sure we would have done our best to cope, but as it is, I can't picture how Mike and I would have done it on our own. How people cope being the only caregiver is beyond me.

TUESDAY, OCTOBER 27, 2009, 5:52 PM

Linda felt stronger than ever today. Her legs felt better and she could get up and walk more easily.

However, her hemoglobin is still low, so tomorrow she gets to have a transfusion, which should make her feel even better pretty quickly. Since they can use her port, it should be fairly easy. We're not sure if this is a one-time thing or will be needed again; we'll have to wait and see.

After the third round of chemo, they'll be able to re-scan her and see what progress has been made, and make any appropriate adjustments. That's also approximately when they'll have a good idea of the effects of the radiation, so we'll be learning a lot in two months or so. Until then, she just has to keep everything going. At her doctor's suggestion, Mike will be picking up some ice cream (the *real* kind) and some instant breakfast so we can make her milk shakes. She did stop at Steak 'n Shake and got a milkshake on the way home today. She said it tasted *wonderful*, but it made her cold, so she's currently in her bed doing what someone called "wrap yourself up like a burrito" to get warmed up.

FRIDAY, OCTOBER 30, 2009, 11:08 AM

Yesterday Linda felt pretty good—the unit of blood she was given helped a lot. A group of her DeVry friends came over and spent a couple of hours with her. They gave her a handmade quilt that had been signed by quite a number of her faculty and staff friends and by students as well—she was quite touched by that.

She's keeping up her Gatorade regimen quite well. In a way it was much better that she was given specific instructions—we all knew it was important for her to stay hydrated, but it's much easier to say, "You haven't finished your second bottle" than "You need to drink more." Maybe she has a little engineer in her—black-and-white limits are so much easier to deal with.

Assuming no more surprises, she has a quiet week ahead—the second chemo treatment isn't until November 10.

She's presently watching a DVD in bed—Dan set up the player and showed her how to use the DVD and TV remotes.

Also, thanks for all the food and drink suggestions. It's amazing how creative everyone is.

SATURDAY, OCTOBER 31, 2009, 9:20 PM

Today was quiet—Linda's leg was somewhat more swollen so she tried to keep it elevated. She had definitely hoped to be more mobile by now, but the fluid retention is still an issue. I guess it needs to be better balanced with her need to keep her blood pressure up. Maybe she can see her doc next week and find a better solution.

As for us: Mike made her lunch, and a milkshake for dinner, I mulched leaves and uploaded the picture of the new quilt, and Dan put the final touches on his latest website blog. He expects to get it up there by Monday.

MONDAY, NOVEMBER 2, 2009, 6:09 PM

Over the phone today, Linda was diagnosed as having cellulite. She called me to say that they were phoning in a prescription for Levaquin and I should pick it up on the way home.

I reminded her that Levaquin is a drug we want to stay away from—it is implicated in torn Achilles tendons and, although it is supposed to be rare, we know, or know of, at least four people who have had that occur. It is evidently less rare in the 60 and over crowd. I found out today that the same applies to Cipro, and there are a number of lawsuits involving both drugs.

So I called the doctor's office and got them to change it. She started taking Keflex tonight and we'll see if that fixes things.

Her spirits will definitely improve if she can walk without pain. Evidently some swelling is to be expected based on the blood clots and the cancer, but red and painful is something else again. I have to be quite gentle toweling her leg off after a shower or I will hurt her. I'm looking forward to that subsiding.

Dan did get his latest blog uploaded. (Video game enthusiasts or good writing enthusiasts see http://www.pixelpoppers.com.) Being able to write has made it easier for him to stick around, for which I'm very grateful. I know he'll have to leave sometime; for my selfish reasons, I just want it to be later rather than sooner.

Previously Linda has been the optimistic one; now my challenge is to help keep her positive outlook. It's difficult because she expected to be getting stronger and feels she isn't; she expected to be more mobile and isn't; and she wants to be able to do some of the simple things she used to do—although she says that I can continue to clean the bathroom and the rest of the house.

WEDNESDAY, NOVEMBER 4, 2009, 7:28 PM

The antibiotic is starting to work. Linda's leg is less red and much less painful. So now we can crack the whip and get her to walk more.

We talked to the oncologist about the swelling and they don't feel they can do a lot right now. They are concerned about getting her blood pressure too low again, and since she's not in the hospital where she can be monitored, they are being conservative. So she will wait until her next appointment on Tuesday.

She was talking about how strange it is to switch gears, from trying to not eat too much most of her life, to trying to figure out how to get herself to eat now. She does pretty well in the morning and then it gets harder as the day gets later; she's more apt to need anti-nausea meds later in the day as well. But at least she is not having the really bad nausea we've all heard about.

SUNDAY, NOVEMBER 8, 2009, 11:46 AM

The last few days Linda has slept quite a bit. She realized last night that the reason she's been so knocked out is that she had been taking a stronger anti-nausea pill, and that was the culprit.

So this morning she went back to the previous medication and made sure to wait a good half hour after taking it before eating. That seems to have worked, although typically she has an easier time in the morning.

I was worried about her sleeping with the bedroom door closed, that she wouldn't be able to call loud enough for us to hear, especially if Mike was the only one home and in his room on his computer. Then I realized that last spring, when we had our garage door replaced, I had kept the old transmitters and the receiver. So I dug those out and wired up a smoke-alarm type beeper to the receiver, plugged it in the living room, and now she has a wireless remote-controlled "call button."

She told me that this was typical of the things one has to put up with when married to an engineer. But I think she likes it.

Later today we'll have a visit from some family members, so I hope she wakes up with some energy.

Tuesday starts chemo round #2. I hope they don't get progressively worse to deal with.

WEDNESDAY, NOVEMBER 11, 2009, 10:46 AM

Sunday was a hard day for some reason—maybe Linda was fighting something off. She wasn't able to get up without feeling pretty bad.

But Monday was definitely better, and Tuesday she woke up feeling pretty good as well. Chemo day seems to go pretty well because in addition to the toxic stuff they give her plenty of anti-nausea medication (which usually lasts for several days).

She also needs to take a steroid the day before, the day of, and the day after the chemo, which has a side effect of making her feel quite awake. So she knows her body is tired, but she still feels pretty good for the first few days of a treatment.

We had a discussion with her doc regarding the leg swelling and blood clots, and his feeling is that there is not much that can be done without unacceptably increasing risk. This is not only for the present; he doesn't expect it to be much improved ever, as the blood clots will tend to clump and stay.

So she has to rethink her mobility options. The more she can keep her legs up, the better, but she would like to get out occasionally, or sit in a restaurant, etc. So we need to find a way she can work with her legs elevated, and she needs to try to walk more. And if we want to take a trip, she can sit sideways in the back seat.

FRIDAY, NOVEMBER 13, 2009, 12:16 PM

After Tuesday's visit with the oncologist, I had to go to work, so I didn't have any time to discuss his comments with her or hear her reaction until I came home. When we started talking about what was said, Linda had already come to terms with some of the issues and, instead of dwelling on any disappointments, was talking about positive steps that could be achieved. I was impressed by her positive attitude and told her later that I thought she was a strong person.

"What do you mean?" she said. "I keep having people tell me how strong I am, but I'm not. All I do is deal with what happens. It's not like I have a choice."

This struck a chord, as I've had people say similar things to me, along the lines of "I don't know how you have the strength to deal with what's happening." My answer had been the same as hers—you just do what you have to do.

But here I was telling her that she was strong for doing that same thing. And when she questioned me, I talked about the fact that she *did* make choices, and the choices were to do things that maximized her options or made the best of what was possible instead of moaning about what couldn't be done. So maybe that's all that "being strong" means. Any thoughts?

TUESDAY, NOVEMBER 17, 2009, 6:13 PM

It's been a few days since the last update, but things have slowed down some. We're more used to the ways our days are structured and how to keep doing our new tasks, I guess.

A couple things have happened. Either by magic, or as a result of the chemo, Linda's legs have pretty much stopped swelling anywhere near as much as they did previously. She is still careful to keep them elevated, but the skin isn't tight and they look almost normal to me (although I never was a leg man). Her attitude now is that if this is the way it will be, it is very livable.

She had a follow-up visit with the radiation guy, and he's ready to schedule her for a CT scan to assess results. She has to get a blood test first to make sure her kidneys can handle the IV dye (chemo is hard on kidneys, which is why she has to keep drinking). But tentatively she'll get the scan on December 7, assuming the oncologist agrees, since he is also planning an assessment around that week or the next.

So we should know a lot by mid December, and Linda is both looking forward to the results and scared of what they'll bring.

As are we all.

In the meantime, we're starting to plan how we'll handle things when Dan leaves, as he must, but hopefully not until after Christmas. Mike is looking into doing more work from home in the mornings, so there should only be a few hours after he leaves until I get home. I have moved one week of my 2009 vacation (the max allowable) into next year, so I'll be able to take her for chemo and follow-ups. And we're mentally preparing ourselves to ask some of our neighbor friends to come over for a few hours when or if necessary.

It's amazing to realize that this whole experience has lasted less than two months so far. So much has changed that the time seems like it should be much longer. We've all learned a lot and many priorities have changed significantly. There have been many good things as a result, although I can't recommend this as the preferred method to achieve them. But there may not have been any other way.

Next week we have the radon mitigation folks come in and do their thing. I hope anyone reading this takes the time and effort to get their house tested. It's very easy and is only $15 for a test kit, and may save you from our experience. If you need more information, see www.radon.com. Good luck.

MONDAY, NOVEMBER 23, 2009, 5:32 PM

Almost another week has passed. Linda is doing as well as possible, I guess, although the chemo is taking its toll. She is having more trouble with acid and nausea, and is alternating drugs in an attempt to help.

She knows this is caused by the chemo, and knows she has to tough it out until that's over, but it's hard to deal with and hard for me to watch.

Saturday was nice so we went out around the pond, and in the evening watched some comedy, which helped. So now

I'm trying to find some more good standup. Until I do we'll go back and watch some old favorites.

FRIDAY, NOVEMBER 27, 2009, 12:15 PM

Linda has asked me to wish everyone a happy Thanksgiving holiday and weekend. She very much appreciates the time you all take to post your great comments.

We had a small Thanksgiving; Linda's sister-in-law and her daughter came over with turkey, stuffing, and gravy. Mike prepared the appetizers, and made cranberries, rolls, and a pumpkin pie. (My contribution was to wash the dishes during the cooking, pour the salad into a bowl, and open the wine. Oh yeah. I also made salad dressing—following Mike's recipe, of course.)

Linda had her usual Ensure and Carnation breakfast milkshake, although she did have a few small carrots with hummus. She's been having stomach troubles, but figured out it was a laxative that had been recommended by her oncologist's nurse that she had been taking the last few days. Having now stopped that, she definitely feels better.

A few more days to the end of the week, and then on Tuesday chemo #3 starts. A couple weeks after that we should get some progress information and, based on that, we'll see what comes next.

WEDNESDAY, DECEMBER 2, 2009, 6:43 AM

The good news: In yesterday's exam prior to the start of the third chemo, the first thing the doc asked Linda was, "How are your legs doing?" When she told him they basically returned to normal, and he verified, he became optimistic, and said he assumed it was because the chemo was starting to do its job. He will check with a scan later, but hopes the scan verifies his theory.

So she will get a brain scan on December 7 and a CT body scan on December 16, and the results will be in prior to chemo #4 (on December 22) so appropriate course decisions can be made. Hopefully, that will still mean she only has to go through three more sessions. Maybe after that's done she'll be able to enjoy food again. It will be nice to be able to eat as a family at some point.

THURSDAY, DECEMBER 3, 2009, 8:16 AM

"All of us here live from scan to scan." I heard that said at a caregiver support group I attended for the first time last night. Like us, some are anxiously awaiting their progress results.

Others have just finished chemotherapy, which, I learned, is the next somewhat scary transition. Chemo was a scary thought at the beginning, but we've learned what is involved and adapted to life during treatment. It is, at least, taking what you hope are positive steps forward.

So what happens when those steps end? What happens when you're not going to be seen, evaluated, and professionally treated every few weeks? I hadn't thought that far ahead until last night. Now, having heard the comments will help us to mentally prepare.

I'm glad I went. I think it will help me. There is a certain level of understanding by people who are sharing the same experience that can't be obtained any other way. It also is a good catalyst for Linda and me to discuss what may occur. My hope is that when chemo is done, and Linda can be less concerned about being out, she can join the patients' support group.

SUNDAY, DECEMBER 6, 2009, 10:40 AM

After some Friday excitement, Linda has been OK. She had been very tired after her last chemo, and around 3 AM Friday got up, went into the bathroom, finished, stood up, and fainted.

Our bathroom is pretty small and luckily she didn't hit anything on the way down. But for the first few minutes while she was sitting there waking up and trying to figure out what happened, I was getting ready to dial 911. She managed to get back in bed, and after we called the oncologist she went in and got checked out. Her blood pressure was OK, but she was dehydrated, so they topped up her fluids and she came home feeling much better.

Looking back, I'm wondering if it was at least partially due to the laxative they had her on the week before. Also, she told me yesterday, they give her some Lasix with the chemo treatment.

In any case, she is more determined to drink all her daily Gatorade, and more if possible.

Tomorrow she gets her brain scan. We don't know if we'll get the results sooner or have to wait for her 12/22 chemo appointment.

SUNDAY, DECEMBER 6, 2009, 7:00 PM

I guess we needed some more excitement, so we spent the afternoon in the ER dealing with constipation issues.

Some good things came out of this experience. First, they did clear up her problem. Second, being in the ER wasn't nearly as bad an experience as we feared. I don't know whether it was the fact that we both came in wearing masks, or it was her history they pulled up, or it was my mention of her compromised immune system, or they just weren't that busy, but they took her right in, and we never sat in a waiting area.

They took a quick X-ray and confirmed no obstruction and treated her. Then after the 45-minute wait to write up the discharge, we were back on our way home, and she was no longer in pain.

The end was certainly worth it. I just wish her oncologist could figure out how to prevent this; we've got a way to go yet. But the ER doc said in his experience this is "not uncommon" and will likely end when chemo ends.

I also learned that we should get the brain scan results when they are available, which should be a few days after the scan.

Tomorrow is a new day—we'll see what it brings.

TUESDAY, DECEMBER 8, 2009, 10:38 AM

Linda just called me with the brain scan results—the brain tumors are GONE. All they can see is a shadow of where they once were.

It's about time she had some good news.

FRIDAY, DECEMBER 11, 2009, 12:15 PM

Other than Tuesday's good news, we've had a reasonably quiet week. That, of course, is a good thing, although it usually means less frequent updates.

Linda keeps learning more about what helps and what doesn't and is continually adjusting.

The next adjustment may be when we get the CT scan results, and after that will be when Dan leaves, which is December 26.

Dan has spent three months being continuously available for Linda and has provided tremendous support to all of us. He now needs to take a break and to attend to his own affairs back in Sunnyvale, so Mike and I need to shuffle our schedules somewhat and learn how take up the slack, and Linda needs to learn what she can do on her own.

It's not something I'm looking forward to, but we've survived this experience so far, and we will figure out how to do what we have to do to continue. I'll be taking some vacation and be off work the last two weeks of December, and Mike will probably take some time off as well, so the real test will begin in January.

One more week and we'll be at the halfway point for chemo.

THURSDAY, DECEMBER 17, 2009, 5:43 PM

I was held up a little at work on Wednesday and got home later than usual, and when the garage door opened, I saw that Linda's car was gone.

Inside, the phone was flashing, and a message from Dan told me that after the scan, they called her back in because they found another blood clot.

It was above the existing filter (which itself had already trapped several clots), and they needed to install another filter higher up. The surgeon who did it was very patient with us and answered our list of questions before the procedure, and also the additional ones we thought of later after the procedure. The procedure itself was a half hour or so, and they kept her in a room for an hour after that, so we were home by 8 PM.

As for the scan itself, the official version will come Tuesday from the oncologist, but we were told that the results were mixed: some tumors stayed the same, some were smaller, and there were some new ones. So Tuesday we'll see what the oncologist says regarding the next phase, and find out if we're truly halfway done, which is mostly what Linda is focusing on for now. She'd very much like to get to where she can eat with us again, or even be in the room while we're eating.

TUESDAY, DECEMBER 22, 2009, 1:00 PM

This morning we got the oncologist's appraisal, which was "Bottom line—this treatment is not working."

So today he started her on a different combination of chemicals. These are supposed to be effective as a "second-line" approach. They are also supposed to be better in terms of nausea. However, it is "a new ball game" which means that the session clock starts over, and after three more sessions (nine more weeks) there will be another CT scan to assess the results.

Obviously, we're all pretty unhappy. Linda, amazing as ever, told me, "We'll get through this too." When I asked her how, to be able to say that, she could say she wasn't strong, she said "I'm not. I just don't have a choice." Since, as part of the therapy, they pump in anti-nausea drugs that last three to five days, she then said her hope was that if these chemicals weren't as bad on her stomach, maybe she'd be able to sit with us tonight while we eat, or even eat something herself, at least until the drugs wear off.

I happened to be able to read the CT scan report, and there were a few good things, such as the lung clot is definitely smaller. But not enough to outweigh the fact the cancer is not homogeneous; some of it responded and some didn't. Some tumors remained the same, some grew, and there are some new ones.

All we can do now is help her get through the next 9 weeks and hope the next scan will be better.

"All of us here live from scan to scan" is certainly becoming our life.

WEDNESDAY, DECEMBER 23, 2009, 9:41 AM

My emotional state is so dependent on Linda. I was depressed when I left her and Dan at chemo. But when she came home, instead of going directly into her bed, she stayed in the living room the whole evening. She had crackers and veggies with some hummus I made the night before (under Mike's direction, of course) and the cooking smells from Mike's enchiladas didn't bother her at all. Mike didn't stop there: for dinner, she had lentil soup and homemade bread.

It was a great night to be together, and made me feel like celebrating instead of crying, which in some ways makes sense and in others no sense at all.

She woke up this morning saying, "I feel fine" in answer to my standard question, where the answer before has usually been "OK" or "Not too bad."

So maybe this drug set will bother her less, and we will have more togetherness. The only difficulty at the moment is that I had bronchitis, so I've been staying away, wearing a mask, and sleeping separately. That should end in a day or so and I'll be able to hug her again—something we both have sorely missed.

THURSDAY, DECEMBER 24, 2009, 6:27 PM

This was truly a wonderful Christmas Eve. Last night Linda ate, but in the living room. Tonight she ate in the kitchen with us all. Mike cooked salmon, green beans, and potatoes; Linda's niece Karyn brought apple cobbler and ice cream; I added salad and wine; and Linda had some of all of it. We also have quite a pile of cookies and goodies brought over by our neighbors, even including a gingerbread house construction kit.

It normally would seem like a small thing, but it was so wonderful to have her there at the table with us. That meal will go into the store of treasured memories that we may need in the future.

And we haven't finished the evening: we traditionally do our present giving on Christmas Eve, so there's more to look forward to.

To all of our wonderfully supportive and caring friends—I hope your Christmas Eve is as wonderful as ours.

TUESDAY, DECEMBER 29, 2009, 3:51 PM

Today Linda went in to check and see how she was doing on the new chemo. Her white blood cell count was low, so they gave her something for that. She's also had some problems digesting, so they gave her a prescription for something that speeds up digestion. All in all, I guess she is doing OK, but it would be nice if these small problems can be remedied. She was pretty tired the first week, but has had more energy the last couple days.

Her oncologist is now suggesting the use of Avastin, starting with, and as an additive to, the next chemo session. Avastin, which has been mentioned in a couple of the guestbook entries, is a biologic rather than a chemical agent. It basically tries to choke off blood supply to the tumors. It is supposed to have a pretty good track record, and if it does its job, she may be able to stop chemo at some point and continue with the Avastin alone.

I believe Linda will go ahead with this suggestion. I want them to do anything that can help, but we know that anything new adds risk, and since we're simultaneously entering a new period without Dan, I know I'll worry more, at least for the first three-week session. After that, according to the doc, we should know what the status quo will be.

The other thing that bothers me is that, although he didn't say this, I think part of his recommendation is based on the fact that things aren't looking great right now; in terms of final outcome, the Avastin won't make things much worse but might make them better. I hope it does.

Yesterday she had some company, and today she'll have some more. Cards keep coming, and even surprise gifts and flowers. Her friends are amazing.

SUNDAY, JANUARY 3, 2010, 12:11 PM

We're almost done with the first two weeks of the new chemo, and we've finally learned what Linda needs to do to keep some food down this time. I guess it's because everyone responds differently to different drugs, but we only get general suggestions from the doc, and have to figure out the specific things that work through trial and error.

At the moment, going back to her anti-nausea pill before eating seems to be the most help.

We've even watched some DVD movies the last couple of nights, as she starts feeling stronger toward the end of each treatment, and it's been a good diversion for both of us.

Tomorrow is the start of the new routine—Linda will be alone for several hours each day, from approximately 10 AM when Mike leaves for work until 4 PM when I get home. We plan to set up a cooler with Gatorade, water, Boost, and whatever else she might want, and we cleaned out the top bedside table drawer and loaded it with all her essentials and with pudding packs and canned fruit.

At the worst, Mike is 15 minutes away, and I'm 30 minutes away. She has our phone numbers as well as those of some neighbors who are potentially within five minutes or less. And there is always 911.

I'll be checking on her during the day, and by tomorrow night we'll have our first impression of how well this will work. If it is a problem, or becomes one in the future, we can hire help.

So that's our happy new year—hope yours will be better.

TUESDAY, JANUARY 12, 2010, 4:26 PM

Today was chemo #2.

We've had over a full week of Linda being "on her own" for about six hours each day, and haven't had any significant problems. The biggest problem was yesterday (Monday, after a weekend) morning when I got her breakfast, got her pills, and when I was ready to leave and asked if she needed anything else, she asked, "Don't I get my cooler today?"

I guess I need a checklist. This would so far include: cooler, frozen water bottles, Gatorade with pre-loosened tops, yogurt (a couple flavors), Boost (a couple flavors), spoon, antacid, ... and if I forget something, Mike can always fill in before he leaves.

All in all, she did pretty well and has felt pretty good the last week, so Mike and I have also felt good.

In addition to the chemo, today she started Avastin. So we have a new set of side effects to watch for, and, I guess, a little more fear about what might happen. We should have a pretty good idea how she'll react in the next few days, and by the end of these three weeks we'll know for sure.

The only issue so far is that she is low in both red and white blood cells, so today and for the next couple weeks she will have booster shots that should help. So far, at least, she hasn't gotten sick, even when I had bronchitis.

And then in five weeks or so, Linda will have another scan. If things are better then, the present chemo will continue for a while, but the hope is to be able to stop chemo at some point and just use the Avastin and possibly Tarceva in addition.

We still have hope.

WEDNESDAY, JANUARY 20, 2010, 3:43 PM

We finally remembered that after the radon mitigation work was done we needed to rerun the test. We ran it the same way as before, and now have a value of less than 0.3. (It was just below 8 previously.) So the fix worked, and we have one less thing to worry about.

FRIDAY, JANUARY 22, 2010, 2:46 PM

Tuesday Linda went in to get what was expected to be a booster to raise her red and white blood count. When her blood was checked, they decided she was OK as is and didn't need the booster. This is a good thing, right? But she was unhappy that she had to make the effort to go in "for nothing" and I found that amusing, which didn't help. Next Tuesday she will get checked again, but at least she's now prepared for either outcome.

Today Linda saw her cardiologist for a checkup. He said everything looked and sounded good, but had her get an echocardiogram to make sure. He also suggested a new medication to raise her blood pressure, especially when she stands up, which hopefully will reduce her lightheadedness.

She continues to battle some nausea and low appetite, and some days are worse than others, but still hopes she is moving forward. Another few weeks and we'll know more after the next scan.

SUNDAY, JANUARY 31, 2010, 4:26 PM

We crossed a couple new milestones recently.

Last week was the first time since Linda got sick that I was gone on business travel for a couple nights. Linda's sister-in-law Chris came over and stayed the second night (thank you again for that) and Mike came home earlier than usual for a couple days, and everything worked out. I even got home several hours earlier than expected, and found Linda sitting in the living room talking with Chris and waiting for me; she said she'd been there quite a bit of the day.

And I know there are some of you out there who might remember a ceremony some years ago involving a pentagram, a knife, incantations, candles, and some cake. For those of you we didn't know back then, this marks our 40th wedding anniversary.

It's unlikely we'll get another opportunity for a while, so my hope is that next week, a day or so after Linda's Tuesday chemo, she'll still be feeling OK and we'll be able to go to breakfast to celebrate. At least it will feel like we did something to mark the occasion (other than the expected hugs, etc.).

WEDNESDAY, FEBRUARY 3, 2010, 1:05 PM

Yesterday was chemo day, the third round of the new drugs, so she'll have a scan in two weeks. That means in three weeks, we'll know if they've helped any, and like before, she's looking forward to the results and also scared.

In the meantime, her hemoglobin was better than it's been in a while, almost up to normal, and all she needed was a white cell booster. The doc's biggest complaint was that she has lost a lot of weight. She still has no appetite, and it's always an effort to eat. But we will be doing whatever we can to entice her. When she came home, she said she wanted real food, and when I asked what, she immediately said "tuna and rice." So that's what dinner was. She doesn't eat a large quantity, but she did have the tuna and also a little salad.

And this morning we did go out for breakfast. She decided she wanted to go to Panera for one of their egg soufflés, and ate about a quarter of it along with a cup of green tea.

She enjoyed being out, and commented on how long it has been and how strange it was since we used to eat out pretty often. I was just pleased that we were there together, and she felt good enough to enjoy it.

This whole part of our lives has only been about four months now, but as Mike said, it feels like it's always been this way.

WEDNESDAY, FEBRUARY 3, 2010, 8:06 PM

A small note on the post mentioning the incantations, pentagram, etc.: No truths were harmed in its preparation.

SATURDAY, FEBRUARY 6, 2010, 12:58 PM

A second small note on the post mentioning the incantations, pentagram, etc.: Two pictures from that ceremony have been uploaded.

TUESDAY, FEBRUARY 16, 2010, 6:15 PM

CT scan was today; now the waiting starts. We'll get the good or bad news in a week.

SUNDAY, FEBRUARY 21, 2010, 9:53 AM

Waiting is getting harder. The closer it gets to Tuesday, the more concerned both of us are getting. Also, maybe I'm just down right now, but the closer it gets the more I expect bad news. And I'm having a hard time facing thoughts about what would be next if that happens.

Even if it's good news, I'm not sure what that means—it would be great to have a miraculous remission or cure, but I don't expect it. And we don't really know what to expect if she is able to get off the chemo—how much energy she will get back, how much mobility, etc.

Sorry that there's no "news" here—I guess I just needed to say these things out loud. I'll definitely update after Tuesday's office visit. We'll see the doc at noon, so the update will probably be late afternoon.

TUESDAY, FEBRUARY 23, 2010, 6:04 PM

First: the scan results.

The doc's word was "mixed." In our case, that means that not all the tumors shrunk or remained the same size. Some shrunk, some grew. The good news: No new tumors were found. And, at least based on the numbers the doc read, the ones that grew did so by a much smaller percentage than the ones that shrunk.

That's a definite improvement over the last scan, where the opposite happened.

However, according to the doc, the results are not good enough to stay on the present chemo drugs. He wants to see non-mixed results. So as of today, the chemo has stopped. He will keep Linda on Avastin and is doing a test to verify that the use of Tarceva is indicated. Assuming that it is, she will start on that as soon as possible. This will be a new experience, as Tarceva is a pill instead of being given via IV.

She is already planning her meals for when she gets her appetite back—steak tacos are first on the list.

This also means she can stop taking some of the meds she's been on—particularly the steroid.

I have to digress for a story. I more or less just came home and wanted to get this news posted. So I made sure Linda was OK, and turned on the computer and began. As I was writing this, Linda decided she was getting out of bed and going to sit in the living room. This is a little unusual in itself. After 30 seconds in the living room, she called out to ask if I had a spare chair in my computer room. When I went in to see what she wanted, she was restless and said she wanted to be with me. So she's now sitting here correcting my grammar and helping me tell this story.

She says, "I'm not sleepy, not sick to my stomach; I have the illusion that I'm stronger (because I don't have to face the chemo side effects), so I can annoy you more."

Second: her response.

A few days ago, we were both scared of what we'd hear today, and Linda was convinced that by last night she'd be a basket case, wouldn't be able to sleep, etc. But that's not what happened. Instead she was pretty relaxed (her pulse today was 72); she slept well; and was not panicky by the idea of less than miraculous results. She told me that one of the big reasons for this was reading all the wonderful posts and letters and cards people sent, and talking to the people who called or came over.

People said (and continue to say) wonderful things. Some of the comments brought me to tears. All these people being so supportive is miraculous in itself, and continues to be a real help. We know that there is help out here in getting us through whatever comes, and, Linda adds, maybe we can have dinner together. (Hope you get the picture she's really happy about losing the chemo.)

And if she stays off the chemo, I assume her hair should start to come back. Don't ask me why, but she said she hopes it comes back red and curly.

THURSDAY, FEBRUARY 25, 2010, 8:41 PM

OK, OK. I guess if I can get used to the no-hair look, I can accept red curly hair.

What I loved hearing (I'm presently stuck at LaGuardia, waiting out the snow) is when Linda said, "Mike made pizza tonight..." pause, pause... then (and I can hear the big grin) "and I had some."

This is better. This is what we hoped for.

TUESDAY, MARCH 9, 2010, 4:54 PM

After waiting two weeks, we got some bad news today. Linda's test results for Tarceva indicate there is only a 7% chance of it helping. The oncologist seems to be leaving it to her to decide what to do—they will find out if the insurance covers it, but then it's her decision, given the side effects.

We also had a visit with a palliative care doctor today in our home. She had some good suggestions that may help Linda feel better in the near term, and will be pursuing those recommendations with the oncologist.

And then there's the ALK drug study. I was alerted to a Pfizer drug trial by my cousin, and the results to date are pretty positive, but Linda needs to have her biopsy tested for compatibility with that approach (similar to being tested for Tarceva) and only 5% of the people tested are compatible. So we'll be getting that test done soon, and then if the results are good, the study is being done through the University of Chicago (as well as other places—we started with the understanding it would be at the University of Colorado, so this is a bit more convenient and there will be more hurdles to go through.

It is amazing how much effort it took to understand how to get her biopsy sample tested—this is usually handled transparently by the doctor involved. I had to learn a lot just to know what questions to ask, but found some helpful people along the way and we're now to the point where I know how to proceed. It was complicated by the fact that it's an experimental treatment, and therefore the doctor can't order the test and have it covered.

If she doesn't qualify, and doesn't go the Tarceva route, there evidently is another chemo to try. But each failure reduces the likelihood of future success.

As the palliative doctor said, you have to keep trying just to "have some peace" that you've tried.

SUNDAY, MARCH 14, 2010, 8:17 PM

The two suggestions made by the palliative doctor have had amazing and wonderful results. She isn't cured, of course, but she feels so much better. She's eating more quantity and types of food, and eating with us in the kitchen. She's walking more, she's awake more, and she's definitely happier.

I am surprised by how much difference seemingly small changes made, and wondering why it took an outside doctor to bring them about. What was the oncologist doing with the list of medications he asked us to provide? Doesn't seem like he was reading it.

So we're happy we started the palliative care, and we'll see what happens next. We hope to get the ALK results in a week, and after that we'll discuss taking Tarceva even though the odds are against it helping significantly, and then we'll see an alternative medicine doc.

THURSDAY, MARCH 18, 2010, 7:28 PM

I continue to be amazed by the change in Linda since changing the meds. Before, I would leave a cooler filled with Gatorade, Boost, yogurt, etc. by her bedside. Tuesday and Wednesday, I was out of town, and Jane and Andy drove up and stayed over. I spoke with her late Wednesday morning after they left and asked if anyone had set up the cooler. She said no, and besides, she was in our family room, and could get what she wanted from the refrigerator. And added, "By the way, can we go out to breakfast this weekend?"

We won't find out about the drug study test until next Tuesday or Wednesday, but we will see the oncologist on Tuesday. So we'll probably just discuss options. If we can't get into the drug study, my preference would be to go for a second opinion at University of Chicago or Rush, or possibly Mayo. More to come....

SUNDAY, MARCH 21, 2010, 11:20 AM

We went out to breakfast this morning, and Linda had her previous favorite—Eggs Benedict. Most of her taste is back to near normal. The exception is bread, which still has a strange taste she doesn't care for. Maybe that's OK, because that's one food that she ate quite a bit of previously; now that she's eating more normally again she needs to be careful because she is still nowhere near as active.

On the way to breakfast, she was smiling, and I told her she seemed pretty cheery. She said, "I am cheery. It's a pretty day, I'm out of the house, I'm not dizzy, and I'm not throwing up." My response: "Good. Sounds like a quote for the blog."

She spent most of yesterday on her computer and we had Thai food in the evening, then watched a DVD movie. Things are closer to normal at the moment, and it feels strange for me to have fewer things that I have to do for her.

But we know that whatever happens, things will not remain static. We're awaiting the drug test results, and will see the oncologist this week and the alternative medicine doc next week, so there's bound to be some changes. And we will deal with them.

THURSDAY, MARCH 25, 2010, 5:19 PM

We just received the news we expected intellectually but so much hoped not to hear—Linda tested negative for the ALK drug study.

So we are getting started on the Tarceva, which will start tomorrow or Monday, whenever it arrives. And of course there is the list of side effects, so her window of feeling good may just have shrunk.

Plans we were considering making will have to wait a bit until we assess how she'll be feeling, which she won't fully know until about a week after beginning the therapy.

It's so frustrating that nothing seems to be able to stop or even slow down this progression.

TUESDAY, MARCH 30, 2010, 8:38 PM

Yesterday we saw the alternative medicine doc. The resulting suggestions are what I would previously have scoffed at, but I now have a new appreciation for the limitations of conventional medicine. And to ease my mind, the doc is an MD, PhD, and Director of Alternative and Complementary Medicine at Alexian Brothers.

So, for those detail-hungry folks (I think this basically means Bob Lawrence, a frequent poster on this subject), Linda is now taking per day: 2-2.5 grams of fish oil with DHA and EPA, 4 capsules of Coriolus versicolor (a mushroom extract, only the hot-water extracted type, of course), 1000 mg of astragalus (an herb), and low-dose naltrexone (4.5 g). After getting her blood test results, she will also be on vitamin D. And she will have a couple sessions of learning how to do qigong breathing. These all are basically to enhance her immune system.

If her next CT scan shows improvement, we will have absolutely no idea what did it, but at least we'll know what to keep doing.

In the meantime, Linda feels good, and constantly surprises me by walking around and actually doing things. She still wants a steadying hand, but she hasn't used the wheelchair to go out to eat or for her last few doctor visits. And her social calendar is full of going out to breakfast or lunch with friends or neighbors or having visitors over. It's great, and it will hit us hard if it ends, but she is so much enjoying feeling better now that it's a delight to see.

The fun continues.

TUESDAY, MARCH 30, 2010, 9:01 PM

One other thing I forgot to mention: She's been on Tarceva now since Friday night, and so far side effects are minimal.

FRIDAY, APRIL 9, 2010, 12:26 PM

In general, as these postings go, each post has usually been triggered by some event. In the beginning, a lot of things were happening, so posts were added quite often. Recently, things have calmed down, so posts are less frequent. But sometimes I feel the need to say a few words even if there is no event trigger. And it does seem that these words are read (which is not required) and responded to (also not required, but very much appreciated by both of us).

So I came up with an event.

Linda has officially reached the end of her short-term disability, and, therefore, possibly the end of her career. Her coworkers and friends aren't quite ready to accept that, however, and have asked her to leave her things as they are in her office, at least for now.

It's hard to imagine that happening anywhere else. What a wonderful thing—to be surrounded in your job by people who care about you. I know Linda cared deeply about her job, her coworkers, and her students. So if a miracle does occur, and she is somehow able to resume her work, it's quite a comfort for her to think she can resume it where she so enjoyed it.

And the various conversations she still has with those coworkers always leave a smile on her face. So, although she deserves all the credit, my continuing thanks goes out to all those people who are keeping her in their thoughts and/or calling, writing, or posting.

TUESDAY, APRIL 13, 2010, 3:28 PM

Had a setback today.

Linda evidently lost her balance at 7 AM in the washroom and started to fall. I couldn't get to her fast enough, and she pitched forward and landed on her nose, fortunately on the carpet.

We immediately called the paramedics, who were great—they got her up and took her to the ER. Of course, when they asked her, she didn't want to go, but luckily they listened to me instead.

She was evidently more dehydrated than any of us realized, and they gave her two liters of fluid. They also started her on an antibiotic pending the result of some blood cultures, which will take 48 hours, to make sure she doesn't get pneumonia. I wasn't happy about the antibiotic—Levaquin—we know too many people who have had damaged Achilles tendons from it—but it's better than getting pneumonia. They also said her nose has a tiny fracture.

So she is now in a regular room at St. Alexius, and I assume it will be for a couple of days at least.

Her oncologist has been by and will be reviewing everything before deciding whether to continue the Avastin, which she was scheduled to get today. But he told her to continue the Tarceva, so we brought that and the other non-standard meds in to the room nurse. Hopefully they'll take care of getting them to her on schedule.

THURSDAY, APRIL 15, 2010, 6:15 PM

So far, all the tests have come back negative. Echocardiogram shows no abnormalities, no infection culture as of yet; blood tests OK, etc. She's at 98% oxygen, so that's not needed.

Still, when she stands up, her blood pressure drops. They are still saying it could be the dehydration, and have continuously been giving her fluids with electrolytes. We don't yet have an anticipated end date. This morning her primary doc said he hoped by tomorrow, but after the orthostatic tests, we know she's not quite ready. They are going to try again before dinner and if she's OK with sitting, she'll eat in a chair instead of in bed.

Mike's coming home soon with a sub and after that we'll go back for a while this evening. I've been loading up her iPod to help her drown out her roommate's evening visitors, who are usually numerous and fairly loud.

FRIDAY, APRIL 16, 2010, 8:33 AM

This morning the primary doc admitted to Linda that he doesn't know why she remains so weak. His next step is to get the team together to discuss possibilities.

She's frustrated at not being able to even sit up without someone being there in case her blood pressure falls, and uncomfortable from being in bed so long.

And I don't what to do to help.

FRIDAY, APRIL 16, 2010, 11:59 AM

Thanks to all for the positive comments—they do help. You can't stop getting your hopes up, regardless of whether they represent rational likelihoods, but we keep being knocked back down. This is certainly the hardest thing I've endured (much worse than when I had prostate cancer) and I'm not the patient. How she keeps being positive is beyond me, but I'm grateful for it. My "rational" outlook on the future is pretty bleak right now.

It turns out "the team" means the cardiologist will be seeing her this afternoon—at least there will be a different perspective.

She was sitting up when I spoke with her just before this post and says she's feeling better—but she still sounds like just talking is an effort. At least she's still trying. I guess we'll wait and see what the cardiologist has to say.

FRIDAY, APRIL 16, 2010, 8:01 PM

Finally, some good news.

When I got to her room, she was in her chair, and had the twinkle back in her eyes. She told me it was too bad I hadn't been there an hour earlier, so I could have watched her walk completely around the nurse's station. It was with the help of a walker and the physical therapist, but she was walking.

The cardiologist more than doubled her medication that helps boost blood pressure and ordered a saline bolus followed by more saline at higher than previous flow rates. She's now down from 250 ml per hour to 150, and she was feeling pretty good the three hours I was with her. And she had already had two visitors over three hours in the afternoon before I got there, so she's come a long way since last night.

She ate dinner, we talked, and we both grinned like fools. She finally got back in bed and said she'd probably sleep the rest of the night, so I'll call her and go back tomorrow.

I've promised her chocolate truffles and Gatorade when she comes home.

They will do some blood tests tomorrow, and maybe take her off the antibiotic, and if anyone deserves anything, she deserves to keep feeling good for a while. And I can finally get some decent sleep.

SUNDAY, APRIL 18, 2010, 12:14 PM

It appears Linda is coming home this afternoon. She is still somewhat weak, and her BP still drops when she stands, but not as much as earlier in the week. They don't really know the cause, although yesterday's blood test showed that her cortisol level is low. Evidently that is a hormone produced by the adrenal gland that helps regulate BP. The abnormality may be due to the tumors, and the cardiologist may be able to find something to help. I spoke with her primary doc this morning, but he needed the cardiologist's consent to let her go home. Maybe tomorrow I can get an update from the cardiologist, and we were scheduled to see him this coming Friday anyway.

We're all scared—Linda's scared she won't get better, and Mike and I are unsure that I'll be able to give her the care she needs. We will be looking for some home care support and, hopefully, talking with the hospital social worker tomorrow, as well as their dietitian, so we can get some idea on how to know when she's had enough fluid.

But so far we've been apprehensive at each stage transition and so far we've managed, which I try to keep reminding myself. It's pretty clear that each stage will likely be harder than the previous one.

Soon they will be delivering a walker and whatever else the home health people have decided is necessary, so at least we'll be ready when she gets home. We've changed the sheets, done the laundry and dishes, and cleaned the house up reasonably (for males, anyway).

And regarding sheets: I know Linda theoretically folded our king-size sheets by herself for years, but now I have to do it, and after much experimentation I can state (and don't forget, I'm an engineer) it can't be done by one person.

SUNDAY, APRIL 18, 2010, 7:42 PM

Well, we made it home. We used a wheeled chair to move her from the car to the front door, but she had to walk in up our too-narrow ramp because nothing wheeled fits on it.

She sat in the borrowed La-Z-Boy in the living room, and we brought her dinner there (Mike's cooking, of course). Then we used the wheeled chair to get to the bedroom, and at the moment she's napping. Later I'll have to wake her for her pills.

She's weaker than I thought she'd be, weaker than I remember her being when we came home from the hospital in October, so this is definitely going to be a challenge to get used to.

But I've been reading the posts to her, and she laughs at some, nods in agreement at others, and tells me how fortunate she is to have so many caring friends.

MONDAY, APRIL 19, 2010, 8:40 PM

We had quite a long night. From being filled up with saline, I assume, she was waking up almost once an hour for bathroom time, which meant I was getting up that often as well to help. Finally it started stretching to two hours or so, and at least she would immediately go back to sleep, but it took me a little longer to calm down each time.

In the morning she discovered that she didn't have the energy she thought she had—she could sit up if she worked at it, but couldn't push herself enough to slide back against the pillows.

So I decided we definitely would need some home help, and called the hospital social worker. He asked whether anyone had mentioned her going to a rehab facility (no one had), and that started the proceedings. Linda was in favor of going because she thought that whereas in the hospital she wouldn't get her strength back, in a rehab place she might.

So she's now there, in a place 10 to 15 minutes from us that the social worker said was definitely the best of the bunch. She seems comfortable and is still mostly optimistic, though she was discouraged for a while today. We'll see how this goes, and if she can't stand it, we'll try to find something else. And maybe she'll come home a little stronger this time, and we'll be able to take care of most of her needs.

TUESDAY, APRIL 20, 2010, 8:27 PM

Linda was still weak this morning, but seemed better in the evening. I asked her her opinion of the place, and the first thing she said was that the food wasn't great—too salty and/or spicy. So I corralled the dietitian and she was very accommodating, said they'd talk with her more tomorrow and make some changes. They also had her primary doc listed as one of his partners, so they got that fixed and verified he will be in to see her Thursday morning.

The nurse assistants respond as quickly as they can, but if they are in a different patient's room, they don't see the call light outside hers. But she seems to be OK, says it's all-in-all a nice place, and doesn't want to change immediately, although I have promised her we'd find something different if she hated it.

They have been pretty responsive, she doesn't currently have a roommate, and she seems to like the physical therapist, so we'll leave things as they are for now.

Now I just have to get the oncologist back on track—she'd like to get back on the Avastin.

THURSDAY, APRIL 22, 2010, 6:11 AM

Things are a little better. Her primary doc came Wednesday instead of today, so at least he is in the loop. And after trying to get an update and prognosis from her cardiologist, we were lucky to find out that her cardiologist's group just began servicing the facility she is in, so he will see her this morning. Maybe there will be some more insight into the cause of her current weakness.

She did tell me that the physical therapist put her through three hours of exercise, including some upper body and even some walking. She came back to her room after that and promptly took a nap, but was awake when I arrived at 4 PM. The therapist has a plan, seems positive, and says it will take a little while but hopes to provide improvement. I was impressed to find out the facility has a large fully equipped physical therapy area, and they must have 15 to 20 therapists on staff.

And insurance concerns that the oncologist's office had have been straightened out. (It took only five phone calls to get them to actually talk to my insurance provider and find out their assumptions were wrong. This is the third time they incorrectly told me that we wouldn't be covered for something.) So, she is scheduled to get back on the Avastin; her next treatment will be Tuesday.

In the meantime I have been interviewing some recommended home health providers so we can be ready for her to come home. So yesterday was somewhat of a workout for me as well. Maybe today will be a little more normal.

FRIDAY, APRIL 23, 2010, 6:31 AM

The cardiologist had an emergency and didn't make it yesterday; he's now supposed to be there Monday morning. At least his nurse called me and explained—I thought that was decent, and unexpected.

She is getting stronger each day—she feels it and I can see it. Yesterday afternoon I was yawning more than she was, a definite improvement in her strength.

Today I'll get an update from her physical therapist, and see her after work as usual.

MONDAY, APRIL 26, 2010, 11:41 AM

Last night Linda seemed down. She said it was because she was worried about how we'll be able to take care of her when she comes home. I guess that will be an issue mostly at night—during the day we plan to have in-home care, but after I come home it will be just me and Mike. If she's waking up a lot at night, getting enough sleep will be difficult.

This also may be where we may have to ask for help from time to time from those many people who have made offers.

But she's getting stronger and, until she does come home, we don't know what things will be like, so there's no use projecting right now.

Yesterday Linda also was "assessed" for eligibility for our long-term care policy. They asked quite a number of questions I didn't think relevant, but got the main issues covered. Assuming she is assessed as qualifying, we'll start receiving benefits after a 90-day waiting period, or sooner if she goes into hospice.

This morning when I talked to her she sounded better, and said that she was stronger in the morning (her typically weak time of day) than previously, both today and yesterday. She's also going longer between bathroom breaks, which lets her think that maybe I will survive her being home. It was good to hear her being more positive.

We haven't heard from the cardiologist yet. We were told he's to be in this afternoon. I'm going to try to get a status report tomorrow, assuming he does show up.

Later today we will be interviewing a home health care outfit that has had some good recommendations. It could be the first of a few, depending on how we like them.

MONDAY, APRIL 26, 2010, 8:50 PM

This afternoon Linda was so much better that I had to add this post. Her cardiologist visited and said there were two possible explanations for her weakness, but the treatment for both was basically what she has been getting, and she definitely is getting stronger. Her blood pressure has, in fact, gone the other way—it's now a little high. But the cardiologist says not to worry, she's fine for now, and if it goes higher they will just lower the dose of the medicine that has been raising it.

Her physical therapist is pleased because she's walking more, getting stronger, and her BP doesn't drop the way it used to when she sits or stands.

The best part: the cardiologist told her it may only be another week or so before she can come home. I was mentally prepared for a longer stay than that, so this is pretty exciting. We just have to be sure we're ready with help when she does come home.

To that end, we interviewed the first home health provider this afternoon, and Linda felt better after learning what would be available. I have one or two more to talk to so I need to get that done soon, I guess.

She had visitors in the morning and in the afternoon, and her spirits were definitely a lot higher than they were the last two days or so. It's so good to see her twinkle has returned again.

FRIDAY, APRIL 30, 2010, 7:49 PM

A lot has happened since Monday's post, and with everything going on I haven't been able to keep this up recently. But here it is.

On Tuesday, we went to the oncologist to resume her Avastin treatments. When we returned, we interviewed a caregiver representative. We liked what we heard. I had been assuming we would have to pay for this ourselves, but the rep suggested that we make sure we weren't covered under our medical insurance, so I did check, and I was surprised to find we do have coverage. The coverage requires care by an RN, and most caregivers have CNAs but not RNs. So we contacted an in-network agency and made an appointment for Friday.

On Wednesday, Linda started feeling nauseous and throwing up. I didn't find this out until I called her after lunch, and she said she was cold and feeling rotten. The CNA had cleaned up her bedclothes and carried them out and then forgot to come back, leaving her with just a sheet. It took a phone call to the management to get things straightened out. She later said that immediately after I called, people began streaming into her room.

They gave her some oral anti-nausea meds, but when I got there she was still feeling pretty bad. After discussions with her nurse, I got them to call her doctor, who ordered IV anti-nausea and saline. The IV did the trick and she was feeling better within a half hour or so and then could sleep.

I think part of the problem was their preconception and/or lack of familiarity with newer drug treatments: they evidently assumed that her nausea was a normal response to her chemo treatment, and it was hard to convince them that although Avastin is under the generic heading of chemo, it isn't a chemical; it doesn't normally cause vomiting; and hasn't caused her to react like this previously.

Thursday was similar: in the morning she wasn't too bad, and even did her physical therapy, but just after I got there she took a taste of dinner and threw up again. It turned out they normally give the anti-nausea medication only if she asks for it, and she doesn't get any advance notice—just all of a sudden feels terrible. So after more discussion, they agreed to do some preemptive dosing for a while without waiting for her to feel bad first.

They also contacted her doctor again who scheduled a blood test for the next morning.

She got her anti-nausea meds overnight and this morning and again after lunch, and when I arrived today she was feeling a lot better. We had to have more discussion to make sure they will keep up the schedule for a little longer, but since it's IV they are concerned about getting her weaned as soon as possible. In the meantime the blood tests came back with everything looking OK, no infections or anything, so they will continue treating the symptoms, which do seem to be abating. We don't know if this was a bug, or a reaction to the Tarceva, or a result of having been on Levaquin and losing her good bacteria. As long as it goes away, and she's not so unhappy, I can calm down again.

We also talked with the in-network caregiver this afternoon, who is going to do everything possible to make sure we get approved for their care and get Linda home as soon as possible. We should find out by the end of next week where we'll be headed.

I'm hoping that tomorrow will be better and this will be over. It's becoming increasingly hard for me to know she is feeling bad and yet be stuck at work. If we do qualify for an RN during the week, she'll at least get individual attention.

Coming up, on the 13th, is a CT scan to see if the current treatment has been any better than the previous ones; we'll get the results the following week. My expectations and hopes are again at odds with one another, but all I can do is wait.

WEDNESDAY, MAY 5, 2010, 11:36 AM

Linda finally started getting better on Saturday, and has been better each day since. She is now back to taking oral anti-nausea meds instead of IV, and feels pretty good most of the time.

She is also continuing her physical therapy and says she is getting stronger, and is definitely walking farther. I'm starting to feel reasonably comfortable about her being at home—still with someone there to help, but at least she'll be in her own place and get back to better food.

We don't yet have a date, but expect to find out soon about the in-home care arrangements, and I will be given an update from her team via a phone conference tomorrow.

She did say that if her next scan didn't indicate progress, she'd probably go off the Tarceva, as that is probably causing most of the side effects.

The question would be what to do then.

MONDAY, MAY 10, 2010, 8:45 PM

Yesterday Mike and I took Linda out in the afternoon. We bundled her up in her winter coat (she gets cold since she's not being active) and took her to a forest preserve and hiked (and rolled her) around a small lake. It could have been a little warmer and sunnier, but she still enjoyed being out for a couple hours.

As of today, we have a tentative coming home date: Tuesday, May 18. Although as soon as I told Linda, I realized that there probably wouldn't be much tentativeness about it—she keeps getting a gleam in her eye and saying, "Tuesday! Tuesday!"

We didn't get approved for an RN, so have arranged for a CNA to be with her on weekdays from the time I leave for work until I get home. We will also have "home health" care with nurse and physical therapist visits as needed.

On Tuesday we'll get her discharged and then see her oncologist and get the latest scan results. We'll be seeing a second opinion oncologist from Rush Memorial on Friday, so she may wait until then to make any necessary decisions.

As always, transitions are somewhat nervous-making events, but I feel like we're much better prepared than when she came home from the hospital three weeks ago. And it will be good to have her home, eating Mike's cooking, sitting in the backyard and telling us what to do in the garden, watching movies together, or just being close enough for some long hugs.

TUESDAY, MAY 18, 2010, 2:13 PM

The good news:

Tuesday! Tuesday! has arrived and Linda is discharged. She is currently at the oncologist's getting chemo, and is looking forward to being home after five weeks.

Her friends at DeVry had a lift chair delivered today. Linda hasn't seen it yet but I know she'll be impressed—it's a power recliner that also will stand her up when she wants to get out. It will definitely be a big help for her. Her DeVry friends continue to amaze me.

The bad news:

The Avastin and Tarceva didn't do as well as standard chemo: since her previous scan in February, her major tumors have doubled. She has now stopped those drugs and has started a new chemo regimen. This will happen on a three-week cycle, with one of the two chemo drugs given on day 1 and day 8 and the other on day 1 only, then repeat. Supposedly the side effects will not be too bad—I guess we'll find out in a few days.

She was definitely disappointed, but is not ready to give up or stop treatment yet. And it will always be her decision that determines our course. But maybe the second opinion guy will have a different suggestion.

I don't know what more to say. We continue to hope and continue to see the cancer ignore any efforts. The continuing support of all her friends is a help—thanks so much for that.

SUNDAY, MAY 23, 2010, 2:02 PM

On Friday we saw the second opinion oncologist at Rush, Dr. Bonomi. He is a nice guy and more caring than her current oncologist, who, we found out, trained under Bonomi.

The bottom line is that everything that has been done so far is fine. He did say that he has a couple patients who are doing quite well on the regimen that Linda is now on even though they have had multiple regimens before that weren't effective. But even if it helps her, it will be an extension, not a cure.

He is recommending that her current doc do a scan at the end of the first three-week session instead of waiting until after the second. If she is doing well (tumors unchanged or smaller) then keep it up. If not, she can see if she is eligible to get into a drug study using Xyotax. In that study she will definitely get the drug. There is also one other study but it's in an earlier phase so there is a one in three chance she would get a placebo.

We can't determine her eligibility in advance since her condition might change, and the rules are strict.

Doing the study would mean going down to Rush for each treatment, but it would still be on a three-week cycle.

The regimen she is on now hasn't yet made her nauseous but she does sleep more than before. I sort of envy how easily she falls asleep.

We've had two days of private care, two different women so far, and she is pretty happy with how it is working out. She also has had visits from the physical therapist and several from the nurse.

She was eating a carrot and managed to dislocate her jaw on one side. She pushed it back into place, but now has to be careful about eating hard things or opening her mouth too wide. (Of course we've already been through all the obvious jokes related to those requirements.) The nurse said that it can happen to anyone and it will take time to heal.

Next Tuesday will be the next chemo. We have gotten used to not being on chemo and have to remember about colds and susceptibility again.

And she loves her chair.

SUNDAY, MAY 30, 2010, 3:47 PM

On the 25th Linda was supposed to get her second part of the chemo, but they couldn't treat her because her platelets were too low (a known consequence of the chemo). So we get to try again next Tuesday. Low platelets, and low hemoglobin as well, so she's pretty weak and tired most of the time. At least she isn't nauseous.

In the meantime, the caretakers have been coming. We've seen three different women so far, and I like two of them, as does Linda, but a different two. One was OK when with her, but according to Mike spent most of the morning (at least until he left for work) watching TV and talking on her cell phone.

The woman I like better sees Linda less often, one day a week, since she works at a nursing home the rest of the time. So Linda hasn't become as used to her yet. But she gives me a detailed picture of what has occurred and how Linda is doing when I get home, and left us her personal physical therapy belt so it would be here all the time. I'll give the other woman a little more time, I guess.

This morning we took her out to the Schaumburg art fair. She started out feeling pretty good, but it was pretty warm and she started feeling lightheaded near the end, and when we came home it was hard to get her inside and lying down. She did feel better later, but is sleeping a lot. I'm worried that she is starting to get dehydrated again, but it's a fight to get her to drink the amounts she should. At least we're having a nurse come in regularly, and Tuesday we'll be at the doctor's office, so if she needs saline she can get it.

TUESDAY, JUNE 1, 2010, 6:08 PM

We tried for chemo again today, but her platelets were lower than last week, so no go. We'll try again in another week, and if they are back up, she'll get a lower dose than the first time.

The low platelets and low hemoglobin are keeping her weak, but she is finally drinking more—I think the way she felt Saturday sank in, so she's not fighting the Gatorade any more. And she doesn't seem to be dehydrated, so maybe we caught it in time. It's hard to know when it's happening—I was told the only way dehydration can be diagnosed for sure is with a blood test.

But she still wants to keep trying. Tomorrow she'll get physical therapy and probably a nurse visit.

TUESDAY, JUNE 8, 2010, 5:32 PM

I came home yesterday and was told that the home care nurse made her get up and walk—I was pretty impressed that the nurse could accomplish that. Linda walked into our family room and sat down at her computer for a while.

Today her platelets were finally up enough to get a chemo treatment. They lowered the dose somewhat so maybe next week won't be a repeat of the last few times.

Her oncologist also agreed to schedule a CT scan sooner—it's now scheduled for two weeks after her next chemo appointment. So if this chemo is doing any good, she will keep going; if not, she will try to qualify for the drug test at Rush.

Sounds like we may be doing lots of driving.

THURSDAY, JUNE 17, 2010, 8:33 PM

Well, I'm guilty of malingering. I'm having a harder time posting because it feels like there are few positive things to say.

Monday we tried for the next chemo, but her platelets were low again. Not as low as the previous time, since they lowered the initial dose, but too low nonetheless. So we'll try again next Tuesday. Either way, chemo or no, she'll get another scan on the 28th; that will determine our future course.

Linda is getting weaker as time goes on. There are multiple possible causes: the specific drug, the disease, and, I was told on Monday, the cumulative effects of chemo over time. Hard to believe it's been almost nine months now, and I think she's only had three or possibly four good weeks in that time. I keep thinking that if I were in her position, I'd be thinking pretty hard about giving up. But you never really know what you'd do until you experience the real thing, so I leave it to her to decide.

And she isn't ready to give up, so we will do whatever we can, whatever has a chance of keeping her going a little longer, as long as keeping going is tolerable.

I've been attending a support group for caregivers, and there are two major differences between Linda's experience and most of the other spouses' experience: most of them are still active (they can drive, shop, etc.) and most of them have some level of constant pain, depending on how "out of it" they wish to be and the level of pain relief meds they're willing to use. At least so far, Linda has not had any significant pain. If that continues for a while (here's where blind hope comes in), it may be a good tradeoff.

It's hard to read more and more about the "miraculous" results of the drug that won't work for her, and just go along with the expectation that things will continuously get harder. But that is the expectation.

So once again I am thankful for the support of all Linda's friends. And I'm trying to hang on to any other good things, however small.

SUNDAY, JUNE 27, 2010, 9:34 AM

Last chemo attempt (on Monday) was a no-go; platelets were low again. Linda's hemoglobin was pretty low, at 8.1, just high enough they couldn't justify a transfusion; she'd need to be below 8.0

Yesterday morning she woke up with some lower abdominal pain. The doc said to get her checked out at the ER, which we did, and she was somewhat dehydrated again, so they admitted her for a couple days. They did a CT scan of her abdomen and pelvis, and everything looked OK. Monday she is supposed to have a CT scan of chest, abdomen, and pelvis, but I couldn't get them to just add in the chest part yesterday. Hopefully they will be able to change Monday morning's appointment from out-patient to in-patient.

It is getting continuously harder for us to get her places. Getting from the bed to wheelchair takes effort for her. I can get her out of the house and to the car using the chair and our ramp, but getting from the chair to the car is really hard.

I have learned an effective technique that is a huge help, but it still takes a lot out of her and takes a while for her to get back to normal breathing, and she has to lie back as soon as possible to become less lightheaded. At least so far her oxygen saturation has been fine—she consistently reaches 98 or 99%. But her heart rate is usually a bit higher than what it used to be, and runs close to 100 most of the time.

The bad:

She is so very weak. I don't know at this point if she is capable of traveling to Rush for treatment, or even how long she'll be able to continue treatment locally.

She is less interested in things. I haven't seen her read or do crosswords (which she used to do constantly). Sometimes she doesn't want TV or anything and seems content to just lie and think. When I've asked her what she's thinking about, she usually says "Not much."

The good:

Except for yesterday morning, she has almost no pain. (And yesterday's pain subsided as the day went on.) She is not nauseous and is eating well.

She likes having me read to her. I started doing this when she was in rehab. We've finished two books so far, and Mike just got the third Steig Larsson book; we'll start that today.

Assuming she gets the CT scan, we are scheduled to get the comparative results on Friday morning. On Friday afternoon the palliative care doc will come out to, among other things, discuss hospice.

Linda continues to want to fight, to put forth whatever effort it takes for even a small chance of improvement. I will help her do whatever she wants, but I don't know how much longer she can put out that effort, and it takes so

much out of her she sleeps the rest of the time. So it's
sometimes hard to see the gain.

SUNDAY, JUNE 27, 2010, 12:03 PM

I just got a call from the doctor on call for Linda's primary
physician. Her hemoglobin is now at 6.5 (most likely due to
dilution caused by the infusion of fluids over the night) so
they will be giving her two units of blood. Her CT scan for
tomorrow morning is now cancelled as an out-patient; they
will decide if yesterday's scan is enough or order a new scan
if not. Based on what I heard, the scan results are what we
feared—this chemo doesn't seem to going in the right
direction either. And they are once again giving her
Levaquin antibiotic for possible pneumonia.

MONDAY, JUNE 28, 2010, 9:40 PM

Today was pretty hard. For all of us.

She had her scan this morning, and, while the lung tumor
hasn't changed much, others have grown, particularly in her
liver.

Her primary doc was out, but one of his partners was filling
in, and she started talking seriously about hospice.

Linda didn't react much for a while, and even signed a
DNR and joked about morphine when it was mentioned
("Morphine. Cool."), but after a while ended up pretty
freaked out, so we got them to get her a tranquilizer, and
she said that helped a lot. The anxiety and fear just
wouldn't let her think straight about anything; even simple
decisions were beyond her for a bit.

I don't know exactly when she'll be coming home, but her hemoglobin is now acceptable, although she is still weak. But she will come home, and we will continue to be with her.

My hope is that she will reach acceptance without too much more anxiety, and that she will remain as pain free as she has been so far.

Thanks to everyone who volunteered to read to her. She liked that a lot.

TUESDAY, JUNE 29, 2010, 12:59 PM

Linda will be discharged this afternoon. Overnight she seemed to come to terms with the situation, and tomorrow we will be talking to the hospice people—she doesn't have the strength to go to Rush and doesn't want to go through any more chemo anyway.

Dan may come in this weekend for a visit, and Linda will be glad to see him again.

TUESDAY, JUNE 29, 2010, 9:37 PM

Well, we thought she would be discharged today, but we were forced to confront a new reality—Linda was too weak for us to get her into the car. And "us" was several of us.

So they brought her back, got her another bed (amazing how fast her spot was filled after she vacated it) and now will stay the night. Tomorrow hospice will meet us there, instead of at our home, and they will arrange ambulance transport. We had a hospital bed and other associated

85

necessities delivered, so this is really the best way to ensure that she is taken care of, and that I don't do her bodily harm trying to get her in by myself. Or harm myself, I suppose.

She is so frustrated. Partially at having to stay another day, but I think it's mostly at how much capability she's lost. It was just a few days ago that we managed to get her out of the house, into the car, and to the ER by ourselves; now we can't handle it.

I keep thinking that once she comes home this time, she's there to stay.

But there are (supposedly) advantages to hospice; care is available (on call, anyway) 24/7, for example.

Many of you who are her friends have posted about visiting, reading, etc., and Linda would be happy to see all of you. The time is here now, and I don't know how long that time will last. And all are welcome.

WEDNESDAY, JUNE 30, 2010, 5:27 PM

Linda was desperate to get out, and after a few mix-ups, we did get her home. The ambulance crew was good with her and she is more or less comfortable in her new hospital bed, which is in our living room.

The hospice admitting people came by and the nurse will visit tomorrow. They also expect to have a nurse's aide visit now and then. It will be good to have someone we can call at any time she has a need.

They are delivering a kit of drugs we can keep and use when necessary—pain killers, anti-nausea meds, anti-anxiety meds, etc. They went through Linda's medications list and told me which ones they will provide from now on. They also provide things like gloves.

So with the private duty caregivers and the hospice nurse, she should be well taken care of during the day. At night, she'll have to rely on me, but I can always call the hospice nurse if necessary.

MONDAY, JULY 5, 2010, 3:54 PM

Linda is sleeping more and more.

Saturday, for the first time since she was initially in the hospital, she had trouble breathing. Hospice had prepared us, so we hooked up the oxygen and it helped. But not enough, so we were instructed to get out her drug kit and give her some morphine.

I've always associated morphine with pain relief, but it also is very useful in helping breathing, and it did help her quite rapidly.

Sunday she needed a little more but it still helped in the end, and it looks like being on oxygen is probably now a permanent need.

This morning she felt nauseous, so I gave her some Compazine, and after a few hours' sleep she said she felt OK again.

It's when she feels bad, and I'm not sure I will be able to help her, that this is hardest. Once she's OK again I'm relieved for the time being, but I know this will more and more be the norm.

Hospice is definitely a help, and I hope they can keep her from suffering up to the end.

Dan has been here since Saturday, and talked with her when he could, but was surprised by how much she sleeps now.

At least when she is sleeping I can feel that she is not suffering. If things end this way, just more and more sleeping and slipping away, I'll be glad.

THURSDAY, JULY 15, 2010, 4:47 PM

Things are progressing slowly. Linda hasn't changed very much in the past ten days or so. She still sleeps a lot, sometimes has breathing issues which are, so far, treatable with small doses of morphine along with a little relaxant, has relatively little pain, and is still eating reasonably well.

What pain she has is often from pressure sores, the result of being bed bound. And occasionally she has an upset stomach.

She has been getting a lot of visitors, which occupies her attention, and which she enjoys even though she sometimes gets pretty tired.

The hospice nurse seems to be very good—she knows what she is doing and is genuinely concerned with helping Linda be comfortable. And the caregivers are very good as well. So I am well supported during the day.

I am waiting for the next change, since it seems like her history is to go along at some level for a while, then something will change significantly, usually for the worse. Like when she went from being able to move around with my help to being bed bound.

The hospice people can describe typical changes, but can't really predict the timing at this stage. They tell me she has an elevated breathing rate and an elevated heart rate, which is usually accompanied by reduced blood pressure as things progress, but her blood pressure is still OK, and she still is eating well.

And for the most part she is mentally alert, understands what is going on, and even responds to my attempts at humor. Every now and then something confuses her, but given the medicine she is taking it's understandable. The nurse told me today that most people know when they are confused and don't like to show it, so they talk less. So far, I think when Linda talks less she is doing so to conserve her energy, but I will be watching a little more closely now.

I read her the posts, and read books to her, and she watches Antiques Roadshow when it's on. And she seemed interested in a Kindle, so now she has one and has used it a little.

Mike is still doing a lot of the food shopping and most (probably all) of the cooking—he's been a great help to both of us, and his presence provides me with the comfort of knowing I'm not shouldering the responsibility alone.

SATURDAY, JULY 17, 2010, 10:54 AM

We learned something important last evening that hopefully will help us understand Linda more.

Every now and then she gets hung up on a word when she wants something.

I asked her if she wanted something to drink, and she said yes. I asked her what she wanted, and she said, "I want a drink that will help me drink."

After my initial confusion, and her repeating the same request, I asked what that might be—water? juice? milk?

She looked at me like, "Crap—what do I have to do to explain this simple request to this idiot?" then sighed, and tried again, repeating the same thing. I finally said, "Do you want something to drink, or do you want medicine?" and she said medicine.

So now I'm mentally going through what medicines we were given, and couldn't think of anything that helped one drink, when Mike said, "Do you want something that will help you breathe?," and Linda said "YES" (with a look indicating that had been totally obvious all along) and sighed in relief that we had finally figured out what she wanted.

Thinking back, this has happened once or twice before, but we were always stumped because we were trying to make sense of her literal words, and never realized we just had to find the right substitute word.

I hope we'll be able to translate better the next time.

THURSDAY, JULY 22, 2010, 5:10 PM

I've been very happy and impressed with our hospice care. One of the best parts for me is that I can call any time, day or night, and I get a nurse to talk to and, if necessary, to come out. So much better than trying to get through to any typical doctor.

Last night I called with a question because Linda started wheezing. As a result, after today's regular nurse visit, a nebulizer with medication was delivered, and later someone will be coming out to show me how to set it up.

In addition, they delivered a high-back wheelchair and a hoist, and said they hoped to be able to get Linda out of bed sometimes. She told them she would like that.

I had assumed that Linda was in that bed to stay, and if they can get her out without causing too much distress, it will be great.

She does have some stomach pain now. It's not all the time but it is getting more frequent, and she is needing a slightly higher dose of morphine to feel comfortable. They tell me she is still at the low end of typical morphine dosage levels, but they are looking for a longer-acting pain reliever so we don't have to wait for the pain to start before treating it.

Her breathing is also getting a little harder, but so far it always slows down a bit when she is sleeping.

We usually see the nurse (who is very knowledgeable, compassionate, and very good about calling me and explaining everything that is happening) twice a week:

Monday and Thursday. But tomorrow we will be seeing the medical director, so the nurse will come along as well.

The medical director is the doctor who took care of Linda when Linda was getting palliative care; she is very sharp and we like her very much.

So I would recommend hospice care to anyone who needs it. Their whole goal is to provide comfort, and I've heard that most people wait too long and thus get the benefits for only a short time when they might have been more comfortable. There are many hospice providers out there, and I've been told in general that the not-for-profit ones are the better ones. Linda is being cared for by Hospice & Palliative Care of Northeastern Illinois. We contacted them because we were given a specific recommendation by someone who used to volunteer for them, and we also heard many other good things about them.

It's a recommendation I hope none of you ever need.

MONDAY, JULY 26, 2010, 10:36 PM

Funny, you would think I would have learned by now, but I had no idea how much harder this would get.

Linda has started having some pain, which has more or less been handled by morphine, but the morphine (I assume) has added a lot of confusion to her thinking. It's usually worst when she's just awakened. Sometimes the simplest tasks leave her repeating the instructions over and over, trying to get a handle on the task, I think. This morning I gave her her morning pills. I usually put them in her mouth and then give her a cup of water. "Drink the water," I say.

"I'm going to drink some water," she'll say. Then when I move the straw to her lips, she'll pull her head back and look at me trying to decide what I'm trying to do. We both repeat what we each said a few times, and don't get anywhere.

Then the caregiver arrived, walked in the door, looked at us, and said, "She doesn't like the straw." This was a surprise to me since she had been using one for the last three days, but sure enough, she ended up drinking from the cup.

So I was able to go to work knowing that her caretaker could handle things.

Tonight we went through the same routine, but she didn't want a straw or the cup, and had already taken the pills in her mouth, so I needed to do something. I kept trying to explain why she needed to drink, and finally she said *"Oh, all right!"* and finished her pills. Then she went to sleep.

But after about 15 minutes she called me.

I asked what was wrong, and she said nothing was wrong. She just wanted to tell me she wanted a half of a mattress.

I asked her where she wanted it, and puzzled over it for a bit, then had a lucky inspiration, and asked, "Do you want to be back in our bed in our bedroom?"

She smiled and said yes, she did, and I should take her there.

It's less often now that she smiles or looks relaxed, but she sure did right then, and I knew she was really looking at me, and seeing me, and being there in that moment.

93

So I had to explain that although I'd dearly love it, we really couldn't get her there, but I'd be willing to lie down beside her in her bed.

And then it was gone, and she was back to being tired, and finally went back to sleep.

TUESDAY, JULY 27, 2010, 8:25 PM

Linda alternates between being "here" and being somewhere else. I wish I knew where that was, but I can't tell from her expressions or comments (which are few); I can only hope it's somewhere good. Though I think her friend is right—sometimes it takes her a lot of effort to parse what is being said and make sense of it.

But every now and then she'll seem to be off somewhere and then surprise me with a response that says she's right here after all.

For a while now, I've tried to frequently tell her how much I love her. We've settled into a little game, where I say, "Do you remember how much I love you?" and she'll nod, usually smile, and say "Gobs."

This afternoon Mike and I were sitting close to her. She had had some pain so I gave her some morphine, and once again she had that far away look. Partly to keep talking, I said, "I sure love you an awful lot" and she turned her head, looked into my eyes, and said, "Gobs."

WEDNESDAY, JULY 28, 2010, 4:32 PM

I think Linda is getting to the point where she doesn't want me to leave her side. When I came home yesterday, I told her I had some messages from her friends to read to her and asked if she would like that. When she said she would, I turned to go to the kitchen and pick up my briefcase; she looked concerned and reached for my arm to keep me there. Once I told her where I was going and why, she let go.

This morning she didn't reach for me but when I explained I was leaving for work she looked unhappy. I asked her if she wanted me to stay home, and she nodded. I reminded her that her caregiver, who she likes, was there; her caregiver said, "I'm here, why don't you want him to leave?"

"He's cute," she answered.

When I came home, the TV was on, and she and her caregiver were watching the news. As soon as she saw me walk into the room, she said, "Hi, baby" and smiled at me. It must have relaxed her to know I was there, because within minutes her eyes were closing and then she was asleep.

With two words and a smile, she can completely melt me.

WEDNESDAY, JULY 28, 2010, 6:23 PM

I forgot one good piece of news: Linda will be getting her first massage on Friday.

I plan to be home; maybe I can get one as well.

THURSDAY, JULY 29, 2010, 4:34 PM

The end is definitely near—I don't know whether it's days or hours, but I wish Linda could just let go. She has basically stopped eating, and drinks little. I hope she will be able to have and enjoy a massage tomorrow, but I don't expect her to last very long.

I'm pretty sure she understands what we say to her, but she has a very difficult time coming up with the words to communicate back. She tries so hard—she'll say, "I want..." and then I wait, and that's usually where it stops. Or last night she said, "Here's the deal..." but I never found out what the deal was.

It's an effort for her to talk, so most of the few times she puts a phrase together, I can't understand what she says.

It's when she says, "Help me...please help me" that kills me. I try everything I can think of, and have no idea if I'm helping. She still smiles at me sometimes, but less often each day. And she still sometimes says, "Thank you" when I do something for her.

In any case, I plan to be here until the end. I will still continue getting support from the caregivers in case I need to go out to get something, or just have a break, but I don't plan to go back to work until she no longer needs me.

FRIDAY, JULY 30, 2010, 7:40 AM

Linda is still fighting, I guess. I have told her all of those things mentioned by so many: that we will be OK, that it's OK to let go, that there's no end to our love for her. Some wonderful friends have, I learned, told her that she didn't have to worry; they would take care of me. To no avail; as of now she still hasn't let go.

Last evening she developed some congestion, so a nurse came out and checked her. Linda's calves are cool to the touch and her extremities are becoming mottled—all signs of the body shutting down. But, to the nurse's amazement, she is still mentally there and responsive. Her responses consist of opening her eyes and sometimes making some sounds, but she is definitely in there.

So about all I can do is keep giving her atropine to clear the congestion, give her morphine often enough to hope she has no pain, and make sure by adjusting pillows and the bed that she at least looks like she is comfortable.

The nurse was just wonderful. She stayed for a while, held Linda's hand, and told her she didn't have to be afraid; we loved her and would take good care of her.

The nurse's estimate of time left, at around 10:30 last night, was a few hours to a day. Linda slept without incident, although I need to keep checking, since there's no way she could call me now.

But after I held her and said good night and told her how much I love her, even with her speech pretty garbled, I definitely heard her say, "I love you too." So I cried my way into our bedroom.

FRIDAY, JULY 30, 2010, 12:32 PM

She is working so hard. But her blood pressure is 80 over unknown, her radial pulse is feeble, her toes are getting blue, and she doesn't respond to having the bottom of her foot stroked—a neurological test.

And while I was writing that last sentence, she died.

FRIDAY, JULY 30, 2010, 5:13 PM

I am so grateful for all the wonderful posts. They meant so much to Linda, and they certainly mean a lot to me.

Linda's body will soon be cremated.

I will post more information soon, but we plan to have a memorial on Sunday, August 8, starting at 11; it will be in Hoffman Estates (not far from our home). There will be food, so I have to have a rough idea of how many people will attend.

FRIDAY, JULY 30, 2010, 9:04 PM

I didn't quite expect such a rapid response.

I have established an email account that I would like to use to keep track of attendees.

Please forgive me if you have already posted your intent, but I would greatly appreciate it if anyone who intends to come would send an email to leumemorial@yahoo.com, specifying the number to be there.

If I can supply a reasonably close count by Thursday, the caterers will be happy. They will be able to deal with some uncertainty but said if I tell them I expect 50, and 100 show up, they will have to scramble.

What Linda desired was that anyone who wanted to would talk a bit—tell stories, etc. I hope some people will want to talk, and I'm looking forward to hearing stories.

SATURDAY, JULY 31, 2010, 11:59 AM

Things are happening pretty fast right now, and I guess I'm not keeping up.

I plan to post an obituary in our local paper and also here on this website, but I haven't finished writing one yet.

In the meantime, for anyone who wants to but hasn't yet sent flowers, in lieu of flowers please consider a donation to Wellness Place, at 1619 West Colonial Parkway, Palatine, Illinois 60067, (847) 221-2400. Or go here: http://wellnessplace.org/donate-to-cancer

They are a wonderful organization and they provide free support for all kinds of cancer-related issues. I have been attending a support group for caregivers there for a number of months now, and there is no doubt it has helped me cope. It also helped me discuss difficult things with Linda, preparing us both a little better for what was happening.

(Author's Note: Sadly, Wellness Place no longer exists.)

SUNDAY, AUGUST 1, 2010, 11:14 AM

Obituary: Linda English Urman

Linda Urman died at home with her husband at her side on the afternoon of July 30, after a 10-month fight with cancer.

She will be greatly missed by her husband Bob, her two sons, Michael and Daniel, and many, many friends.

Linda grew up on a farm in Bloomington, Illinois. She received her B.A. in 1970 at the University of Illinois and her Master's degree in English Literature from Northwestern in 1971. After raising two sons, she went back to school and received her teaching degree, and eventually became a Senior Professor at DeVry University.

In 2008, she received her Ed.D in Adult Education.

She loved teaching, and cared for her students, and touched many lives in a positive way. She received that love back many times over during her illness.

Linda and Bob celebrated their 40th wedding anniversary earlier this year.

A private cremation and memorial will be held.

In lieu of flowers, donations to Wellness Place are appreciated (http://wellnessplace.org/donate-to-cancer).

MONDAY, AUGUST 2, 2010, 9:26 PM

The obituary I previously posted will appear in our local paper, The Daily Herald (http://www.dailyherald.com) tomorrow and Wednesday.

If anyone needs directions to the memorial, please let me know via email at leumemorial@yahoo.com.

Again please accept my thanks for the wonderful comments. My responsibilities have basically ended, and I'm not quite sure what to do with myself now, but reading these posts, while sometimes hard, helps.

Michael has been so wonderfully supportive and helpful, and I hope I have been as supportive to his needs as he has to mine. Luckily, he has a good relationship with a caring woman, and I know she has been a great source of comfort to him.

I also have been blessed with a wonderful sister-in-law, Chris, who understands all too well the experience I'm going through, and has been so supportive to me and to Linda. She hopefully will continue being my guide for a while longer.

And so many friends have offered their unconditional help.

There is nothing that can compete with these riches.

THURSDAY, AUGUST 5, 2010, 4:21 PM

One important reminder about the memorial—it is <u>not</u> formal.

THURSDAY, AUGUST 5, 2010, 12:30 PM

Looking back at all the posts written by so many others, one thing seems clear.

This is what matters in life:

- To treat people with dignity, kindness, and respect.

- To help each other when needed.

- To have and keep friends.

- And to love unconditionally.

Linda just always did that, because that's who she was. And it has come back so many times over.

THURSDAY, AUGUST 5, 2010, 9:46 PM

A question has come up regarding the memorial. If I've been too vague or confusing, I didn't mean to be.

Anyone is welcome to come when they wish, but there is somewhat of an agenda, so there is a more or less defined starting time. Anyone who wishes to take part in the event from the start should plan to arrive at 11 AM or not too much later. It will take some time to greet people as they arrive, so there is that flexibility. There will be a buffet lunch which will be available starting around 11:30, and I plan to say what I'd like to say not long after that. Then it will be open to anyone who wishes to speak, and we'll see how long it lasts. We will need to done by 4 PM.

I hope this helps.

SUNDAY, AUGUST 8, 2010, 12:00 PM

Eulogy

First I'd like to express some thanks.

To all the people who called, visited, and sent numerous cards,

To all the people who posted their sympathies, suggestions, and good wishes,

To all the people who just kept Linda in their hearts,

And to the people who are here today:

Thank you so much.

We are here for a couple reasons.

The obvious reason is because of our various connections to Linda, and because she asked me to do this for her.

Linda has touched many lives, some tangentially, some profoundly. She always was one who gave, and that giving has been returned many times over by you, her friends.

The other reason we are here, I believe, is because we hope this will help us deal with losing her.

Somehow, this will help us accept the finality, and help us let go.

What Linda wanted was an opportunity, for anyone who wishes, to talk: tell stories, reminisce, whatever is helpful for them and maybe for the rest of us.

So, since I actually have been asked to, I thought I'd start by talking a little about her history and our life together.

I've written it out so I won't forget anything and in case I can't get through it, so please excuse my reading it to you.

Then, if anyone wishes to add anything, please do. I'm sure there are many stories I haven't heard, and I'm very much looking forward to hearing them.

- - -

Linda grew up on a farm in Bloomington, Illinois. She had an enjoyable childhood and did things that most of us city folk haven't, such as riding pigs in her yard and plucking chickens. She learned a lot as well. Among many other things, she learned to drive a tractor and a stick-shift pickup truck at an early age.

As an aside: the first car we bought had a manual transmission, and after a year the car developed a serious engine defect, so we sold it. When the buyer asked why we were selling it, I told him it was because it had a manual transmission and my wife was tired of not being able to drive it. I'm not sure she ever fully forgave me for that.

One of the main things she learned growing up was that she did not want to be a farmer's wife. When it came time for college, she was determined not to go to the local university, and instead went to U of I in Champaign, majoring originally in botany and minoring in psychology. Not long after she started the semester, she became friends with a woman who knew me and thought we would get along, and who fixed us up.

I had one of the early Honda motorcycles, a 65cc toy, really, and years later I found out that it was the motorcycle that intrigued her and clinched the decision.

As only a somewhat calculated move, our first date was to a Mozart opera. I guess that and the motorcycle did the trick, and we kept dating, but as friends, since I had a girlfriend back home. So we'd shake hands goodnight. She hadn't had much exposure to classical music, which was most of what I listened to in those years (until her brother corrupted me with the Beatles and the Stones) so I brought her that experience, and she tried to open my eyes to various botanical things. She learned to enjoy Shostakovich, Bach and others; I still categorize plants as either flowers, trees, or grass.

After my back-home girlfriend decided to end it, Linda and I started dating more conventionally. As we got to know each other better, I wanted to have more and deeper communication. Linda had been used to spending time alone when she was on the farm, and wasn't sure if she was ready to fully open up with me, or anyone, I guess. One day when we were out on my newer and bigger motorcycle, I got frustrated, drove back to her dorm, and gave her a choice: talk to me or get off the bike. She made a decision, didn't get off, and we've talked ever since.

When we met, I was in my third year out of the five years it took me to finish; she had started with advanced placement credits, and so she ended up graduating one semester after I did. During her last semester I convinced her to marry me, and within a few weeks of her graduation we were married and had moved to our first apartment.

To clear up any confusion regarding some cryptic comments about our wedding ceremony:

We had two ceremonies. The second was the "official" ceremony. It was held in her parents' farmhouse, and was more or less traditional.

The evening before, however, we held a non-official ceremony, planned by one of our close friends at that time. It may sound strange as I first describe it, but bear with me.

We had a ceremony book that contained readings, a small table that held a bowl and some ingredients, and the floor was covered with a large plastic sheet on which a pentagram with inscribed circle was drawn, with one segment of the circle left open.

The basic idea was drawn from early history, and had to do with demons.

It turns out that individuals are most vulnerable to demons at the point at which they are newly born. Since a wedding is a joining of two individuals into one, that new individual is also vulnerable. So the goal is to shield the new married couple/individual from the sudden new vulnerability.

Step one is to confuse the dumber demons. So we made a show of leaving the house by the front door, and snuck around to the back door where we re-entered, with me last, backing in, and (step two) holding a knife to scare off the more timid demons. We entered the circle in the pentagram at its open segment, which was immediately closed (via magic marker, of course).

By this time we've lost the weaker demons and are now protected by the pentagram, and the stronger demons are getting confused about how to get to us.

For step three, our friends, who are surrounding the pentagram, come up to the small table in pairs. One selects an ingredient, and puts it into the bowl, mixing when necessary. The other reads the appropriate incantation from the ceremony book. Each incantation addresses a specific demon—the demon of jealousy, the demon of self-indulgence, and so on. These demons, already confused, become so anxious to get to us that they instead end up mixed in to the cake that is being assembled by the ingredients in the bowl, and one by one get permanently caught and baked in at the end.

Now we have a truly demonic cake, which would be harmful to us in our vulnerable state if we had even a bit of it. To prevent that, the cake is shared by our friends, each taking a small piece so no great harm will befall them, thereby protecting us from the total harm we were vulnerable to.

Now the best part comes: Protected, we leave the pentagram, and read the last part of the ceremony, the benediction, where we thank all our friends for sharing among them the burdens we would otherwise have needed to shoulder alone, and remind them that, as we are now under a protective umbrella, they should join us often, where they will be under that umbrella as well.

I'm pretty sure it was unanimous that the cake was awful.

But many of you here today were with us then, and we always were grateful for our long friendship.

Linda had been given a stipend and a full scholarship at Northwestern to work towards master's and doctorate degrees in English Literature, and so she went to school, worked on her thesis, and learned to cook for us while I worked at my first job as an engineer. She received her Master's but was disillusioned with Northwestern's culture, so she went to work full time and became a claims analysis specialist and manager for Social Security. She learned a lot about dealing with people by putting her psychology training to use.

We were married about eight years when she decided it was time to have kids, and Michael was born in 1979. (He arrived a month early—her water broke when she was walking to work in downtown Chicago, so she got on the train, came home, and drove herself to the hospital. I only found out when a nurse called me at work.) She then became a full-time mom, and never again wanted to be a manager.

A few years later she convinced me it would be OK to have more than one child, and Dan arrived. This took some convincing, as, due to my personal history, I was worried that my kids wouldn't get along. So she set us up for marriage counseling, which helped greatly, and she clinched the deal by saying that if we had the second kid, she'd get her tubes tied; if not, I'd have to get a vasectomy.

She was the one who did the research and decided how we would discipline our kids, and taught me both the theory and techniques and the importance of consistency and a united front. And I believe it worked out: our kids get along. And when Dan was in college he took a psych class that evidently discussed child-raising and discipline

108

techniques, and he told us he was impressed to find that we had done everything by the book.

So our kids grew up into independent and successful adults, and this year we celebrated our 40th anniversary.

She finally decided it was time to go back to work, so she went back to school and got her education degree, assuming she would teach in high school. But I had moved to a new job, and my cubical mate was a part-time teacher at DeVry who suggested she look there for an opportunity, and she did so. She started as an adjunct and in a short time was offered a full-time position. In the meantime, my cubical mate had decided to quit his engineering job and teach full time as well, and he then became Linda's first cubical mate in her new job.

She genuinely liked people and it came across—she really cared about making her students successful and her students responded. I'm sure it was a factor in her success as a teacher, and it was reflected in the many positive comments on RateMyProfessor.com.

She found a wonderful environment at DeVry, and was very happy teaching where she could do what she believed in and found so much support from her peers. The encouragement and support of one of her peers led her to put in the long effort that resulted in receiving her Ed.D. Her advisor, who all along the way was helpful and very supportive, said her dissertation contained "pioneering research" that he expects to frequently be cited in the future. He has also asked for and received Linda's permission to publish the core of her dissertation as an article.

So many people cared so much for her. You, her friends, have been so supportive. And she very much appreciated the visits, the posts, the cards, and the calls, and the knowledge that she touched so many lives.

For my part, Linda has brought me and taught me so much. She always has been very giving and very empathetic. She liked the Meyers-Briggs framework and told me that it helped her understand and deal appropriately with some of the differences between us. It took her a while to understand that, while she was the type who thinks about things and then states her opinion, I often think by expressing my thoughts out loud, continuously revising my pronouncements until I reach my conclusion. Before she analyzed and understood that, I had evidently confused her pretty regularly.

When I was younger, I wondered how I had been so lucky as to snag such a beautiful woman. Later, I wondered how I had been so lucky as to snag such an incredible and compatible partner—beautiful, intelligent, compassionate, and loving.

Since I knew all the things Linda had brought me over the years, I recently asked her to tell me what I had provided to her. Her answer: "Just the way you look at me is enough."

When I was younger, I wasn't sure if I knew what "love" really was. Now I know, and am so grateful to Linda for helping me learn.

I will end this with the benediction from our first wedding ceremony.

BENEDICTION

May all who rest within our home share this charm which you have laid upon us.

In the measure that you share our burdens, so also may you share our fortune.

As our shadows fall upon you now, so may our light in time to come.

As you eat this cake, which we may not, so may you break bread with us ere journey's end.

Acknowledgements

Our sons, Mike and Dan, were incredibly helpful—to Linda, certainly, and to me as well.

Dan, as soon as he heard what had happened, left his home in California, flew in, and stayed with us several months, taking care of Linda so Mike and I could continue going to work. He entertained her, drove her to appointments, and kept her company when she was in the hospital for procedures and then when she came home. Linda told me how glad and relieved it made her feel to have him with her, and appreciated everything he did for her.

Mike, who was living at home at the time, went to work, then shopped, cooked for us all, and supported me at a time when we both needed a lot of support. (We both did a fair amount of crying, a lot at the beginning, and then again at the end.) He helped me every step of the way; I only can hope I helped him as well.

Debbie, Mike's girlfriend (and now his wife), gave Mike the external support he needed to keep going. It's hard to know how he would have coped without her, and I'm grateful we never had to find out. She also did a great job of editing this book.

Chris, my sister-in-law, having lived through a similar experience with her husband, was my guide. She visited Linda regularly, stayed with her when I had to travel overnight for my job, and provided that deep understanding of what we were going through that only someone who had experienced it could know.

Jane, Linda's "almost sister," made the long drive from Missouri several times to talk with Linda and spend time with her.

A special thanks goes to Kathy Scortino, a registered nurse and clinical counselor who led two support groups I regularly attended at Wellness Place—initially, a caregivers' support group, then later, a bereavement support group. Her empathy and insightful comments and suggestions went a long way in helping me cope, and the groups provided a supportive environment unmatched anywhere else.

Another special thanks goes to my sister Ruth, an author, who also helped edit this book and provided many good suggestions to improve clarity. Her works may be seen here: lifeathideawayhaven.wordpress.com.

Our friends and Linda's coworkers were extraordinary. So many people posted their good wishes, their suggestions, their jokes, and their sorrow. She taught at DeVry, and I was told that there had never before been such a level of concern and sympathy from so many teachers and students. The posts were a continual source of comfort to Linda, and I read them to her to the end. Including their posts in this story would have added over 300 pages; anyone wishing to see them can do so here:

http://www.caringbridge.org/visit/lindaurman/guestbook

Note that the posts are, by default, sorted from newest to oldest. This can easily be changed using the *Sort:* dropdown menu.

One last mention: To Barb, wherever you are: Thank you for fixing us up those many years ago. Because of your efforts, I met a beautiful girl who turned into an exceptional woman and gave me 43 years of companionship, love, support, and true partnership.

www.ingramcontent.com/pod-product-compliance
Lightning Source LLC
Chambersburg PA
CBHW071201280526
45787CB00002B/566